Soups

Soups

Edited by Anna Horn

STERLING
INNOVATION
A Division of Sterling Publishing Co., Inc.
New York

Library of Congress Cataloging-in-Publication Data Available

2 4 6 8 10 9 7 5 3

Published in 2007 by Sterling Publishing Co., Inc.
387 Park Avenue South, New York, NY 10016

Originally published as *Quick Cooks' Kitchen: Soups*
This book is comprised of material from the following Sterling titles:
365 Vegetarian Soups © 2002 by Gregg R. Gillespie
Smart Soups © 1998 by Carol Heding Munson

© 2004 by Sterling Publishing Co., Inc.
Photographs © 2004 by Theresa Raffetto

Distributed in Canada by Sterling Publishing
c/o Canadian Manda Group, 165 Dufferin Street
Toronto, Ontario, Canada M6K 3H6
Distributed in the United Kingdom by GMC Distribution Services
Castle Place, 166 High Street, Lewes, East Sussex, England BN7 1XU
Distributed in Australia by Capricorn Link (Australia) Pty. Ltd.
P.O. Box 704, Windsor, NSW 2756, Australia

Design by Liz Trovato
Photographs by Theresa Raffetto
Food Stylist: Victoria Granof
Prop Stylist: Sharon Ryan

Printed in China
All rights reserved

Sterling ISBN-13: 978-1-4027-4349-8
ISBN-10: 1-4027-4349-1

For information about custom editions, special sales, premium and
corporate purchases, please contact Sterling Special Sales
Department at 800-805-5489 or specialsales@sterlingpub.com.

Contents

Introduction

With so many options for a quick meal—quality frozen, prepped, and ready-to-heat foods; take-out, delivery, and microwavable everything—there seems to be little reason to cook! *Soups* provides you with more than 170 recipes filled with home-cooked goodness to satisfy the busy chef in us all.

Soup is a wonderful soul-warming food that brims with wholesome ingredients and fantastic flavors. Indeed, soup is the epitome of comfort food. Chicken soup is the elixir of choice when a cold or flu has you feeling down. Soup fills you up, yet can be so healthfully light in fat, carbs, and calories, that it may be a dieter's dream. There are endless reasons why soup holds a special place in our menu repertoire. A fragrant and delicate soup can stimulate the appetite, serving as a perfect opener to a dinner. A robust, stick-to-the-ribs soup, served with crusty bread and a salad, makes the perfect one-dish meal.

Even with all of its benefits, many people shy away from making soup for one of these reasons: It takes too much time to cook—rumor has it at about eight hours of simmering! Or, it requires too big a pot—a gigantic one that must hold 10 to 12 quarts, and you must have expert culinary skills. *Soups* is all about debunking such myths—all-day simmering, space-gobbling equipment, and the aptitude of a professional chef are definitely not on this cook's list.

In this book, you'll see recipes for a wide variety of soups: some ready to eat in an hour or so; some ready in mere minutes. Some have international origins; some are decidedly domestic. Whether you have time to spend in the kitchen, need a quick dinner fix, or want some super–smart cooking tips to help you along—you have chosen the right cookbook.

Cooks' Tips

It is an hour or two before dinner and you are craving a comforting homemade soup. It has been a hectic day, and now you would really like to unwind with something that has the power to soothe your soul, perk up your mood, and be shared with your family and friends. Soup is the only answer. If you are wondering how you can put a meal on your table with relative ease, here are some tips:

• Use commercial broth and beans. Many store-bought products contain high sodium content so check for low-sodium products, and rinse canned beans before cooking. Then season to taste—that way you are in control of just how salty your dish is. Having said that, we have also provided basic soup stock recipes on pages 9–10. If you ever have the time to cook up some stock, simply freeze 1- and 2-cup quantities for use when the mood hits you.

• Chop your ingredients smaller rather than larger and try for uniformity in the size. This will lend itself to quicker, more even cooking.

• Most soups are one-pot affairs, so clean-up can be a snap, which gives you more time to enjoy.

• Read the recipe from start to finish before beginning your prep. Make sure you understand the directions and reread anything that seems unclear.

• Start by getting all of your ingredients within reach and do all of your prep work before beginning to cook. That way, you can cruise through the instructions and simmer up a great soup.

Basic Tools

You can create any of the soups in this book with just a few basic kitchen tools:

Cutting board: At least one board in either wood or plastic is a must-have. Whichever you choose, be sure to get one large enough for unhindered chopping, yet small enough for easy washing. For food safety, remember to use separate boards (or separate sides of one board) for cutting produce and raw meats and to wash the boards thoroughly between uses.

Chef's knife: Select a top-quality knife and keep it sharp for optimum performance. This knife comes in 6-, 8-, 10-, and 12-inch lengths. The 8-inch one gets our vote for versatility. It lets you cut meats, chop vegetables, and mince garlic and herbs in no time flat.

Paring knife: A paring knife usually comes with a 3- or 4-inch blade and makes short work of trimming mushrooms, peeling fruits, and other similar tasks.

Vegetable peeler: This tool is ideal for peeling thin-skinned root vegetables such as carrots, potatoes, parsnips, and even young butternut squash. Find a peeler with a swivel blade and a comfortable handle.

Measuring cups and spoons: Get a nested set of dry measuring cups for measuring rice, pasta, beans, and frozen peas and corn. Use a liquid measure for broth, tomatoes, and other liquid ingredients. One set of nested spoons can be used for dry and wet items.

Wooden spoons: Wooden spoons are good for most mixing and stirring tasks. They don't scratch pots, pans, or dishes, and their shallow bowls are perfectly suited for stirring. Their handles stay cool, and don't melt if you accidentally leave them touching a hot pot.

Large metal spoons: A good-sized spoon with a deep bowl is ideal for stirring chunky, hearty soups.

Ladle: A ladle with a half-cup capacity is great for serving chowders and soups with a lighter base.

Saucepans and pots: The saucepan is the smaller of the two and has one handle; the pot is larger and has two handles. All of the soups can be made in either vessel. The pot, however, will give you more room for stirring and gentle simmering. Make sure you get a snug-fitting lid for whatever you have. The pot itself should be heavy and a nonstick interior is not necessary.

Immersion blender: This handy gadget allows you to purée ingredients directly in the pot. If you don't have one, a blender, food processor, food mill, or potato masher will work.

Soup Stocks

PREP TIME: 15 MINUTES   COOK TIME: 2 HOURS 10 MINUTES

Beef Stock

MAKES 9 CUPS

A lean stock that's rich and flavorful.

nonstick spray
2 ribs from roasted beef rib roast
2 celery stalks, leaves included, halved
4 large onions, with skins, quartered
4 medium carrots, halved
2 small turnips, quartered
2 bay leaves
8 whole black peppercorns
1 sprig parsley
1 sprig rosemary
10 cups water

• Coat a nonstick skillet with the spray and warm it over medium-high heat for 1 minute. Add the beef ribs and cook them until the pieces are browned on all sides. Transfer the ribs to an 8-quart pot. Add the celery, onions, carrots, turnips, bay leaves, peppercorns, parsley, rosemary, and water. Cover the pot, and bring the mixture to a boil. Reduce the heat, and simmer for 2 hours.

• Pour the stock through a large strainer into a large bowl or pot. Discard the beef bones, vegetables, and seasonings. Chill the stock; then skim and discard the fat that's accumulated on top of the liquid.

PREP TIME: 15 MINUTES   COOK TIME: 25 MINUTES

Vegetable Stock

MAKES ABOUT 9 CUPS

The tastiest vegetable stock I've ever tried, and it's exceptionally easy to make.

4 large onions, quartered
4 medium carrots, halved
4 celery stalks, leaves included, halved
10 basil leaves
2 bay leaves
2 cloves garlic
8 whole black peppercorns
1 sprig parsley
10 cups water

• Combine the onions, carrots, celery, basil leaves, bay leaves, garlic, peppercorns, parsley, and water in an 8-quart pot. Cover the pot, and bring the mixture to a boil. Reduce the heat, and simmer for 25 minutes.

• Pour the stock through a large strainer into a large bowl or pot. Discard the vegetables and seasonings.

PREP TIME: 20 MINUTES   COOK TIME: 1 HOUR 15 MINUTES

Chicken Stock

MAKES ABOUT 9 CUPS

A fast-to-make stock with only 1 gram of fat.

olive-oil nonstick spray
1 pound bone-in chicken breasts
2 celery stalks, leaves included, halved
4 large onions, with skins, quartered
4 medium carrots, halved
1 small turnip, quartered
2 bay leaves
8 whole black peppercorns
1 sprig parsley
1 sprig thyme
10 cups water

• Coat a nonstick skillet with the spray and warm it over medium-high heat for 1 minute. Add the chicken and cook it until the pieces are browned on all sides. Transfer the chicken to an 8-quart pot. Add the celery, onions, carrots, turnip, bay leaves, peppercorns, parsley, thyme, and water. Cover the pot, and bring the mixture to a boil. Reduce the heat, and simmer for 1 hour.

• Pour the stock through a large strainer into a large bowl or pot. Discard the chicken bones, vegetables, and seasonings; reserve the chicken breast meat for another use. Chill the stock, then skim and discard the fat that's accumulated on top of the liquid.

PREP TIME: 15 MINUTES   COOK TIME: 1 HOUR 10 MINUTES

Turkey Stock

MAKES ABOUT 9 CUPS

A great way to use up leftover turkey wings.

2 roasted turkey wings, skin included
2 celery stalks, leaves included, halved
3 large onions, with skins, quartered
2 medium carrots, halved
1 small turnip, quartered
1 parsnip
2 bay leaves
8 whole black peppercorns
1 sprig parsley
1 sprig sage
10 cups water

• Combine the turkey, celery, onions, carrots, turnip, parsnip, bay leaves, peppercorns, parsley, sage, and water in an 8-quart pot. Cover the pot, and bring the mixture to a boil. Reduce the heat, and simmer for 1 hour.

• Pour the stock through a large strainer into a large bowl or pot. Discard the turkey, vegetables, and seasonings. Chill the stock; then skim and discard the fat that's accumulated on top of the liquid.

COOKS' TIP:

To store the stock, refrigerate it in covered 2-cup containers for up to 3 days, or freeze it for up to 3 months.

Right: Cold Dilled Tomato Soup.

Cool Vegetable Soups

Delicate Vichyssoise with •
Roasted Peppers
Cucumber-Parsley Soup •
Cold Dilled Tomato Soup •
Chilled Carrot-Orange Soup •
Chilled Guacamole Soup •
Chilled Cucumber Soup •
Fast Gazpacho •
Sweet & Spicy Carrot Soup •

• Chilled Tomato Basil Soup
• Avocado & Spinach Soup
• Chilled Red Pepper Soup
• Chilled Cream-of-Vegetable Soup
• African Tomato & Avocado Soup
• Arugula Soup with Tomato Salsa
• Curried Apple & Carrot Soup
• Chilled Pea Pod Soup
• Asparagus & Vegetable Soup

PREP TIME: 20 MINUTES   COOK TIME: 20 MINUTES, PLUS 1 HOUR TO CHILL

Delicate Vichyssoise with Roasted Peppers

MAKES 6 SERVINGS

Never had vichyssoise (pronounced vee-she-SWAHZ)? It's a potato-leek soup traditionally served cold and topped with minced chives. Now is a great time to give it a try. This version is coolly sophisticated, ultra-light, and extra easy to make.

2 teaspoons butter
2 large leeks, white parts only, chopped
2 large waxy potatoes, peeled and diced
1 can (14 ounces) fat-free chicken broth
1/4 teaspoon white pepper
1/4 teaspoon celery seeds
1 teaspoon white wine vinegar
2 cups 2% milk
1/4 cup chopped roasted red peppers

• Melt the butter in a 6-quart pot over medium-high heat. Add the leeks, and cook until they are translucent, about 5 minutes. Stir in the potatoes, broth, pepper, celery seeds, and vinegar. Cover the pot, and bring the mixture to a boil. Reduce the heat, and simmer for 15 minutes. Remove pot from heat; let the mixture cool, uncovered, for 2 minutes. Transfer the mixture to a blender jar. Process until puréed.

• Pour the mixture into a large bowl, stir in the milk, and chill the soup thoroughly, about 1 hour. Top each serving with peppers.

COOKS' TIP:

Roasted peppers from a jar work very nicely in this soup. Just be sure to drain them.

PREP TIME: 10 MINUTES   COOK TIME: 20 MINUTES, PLUS 1 HOUR 10 MINUTES TO CHILL

Cucumber-Parsley Soup

MAKES 4 SERVINGS

This summertime refresher is truly "cool as a cucumber." Fresh parsley and dill make it extraordinary.

2 teaspoons canola oil

1/2 cup chopped onion

2 cups fat-free chicken broth

2 cups diced cucumber

1 cup diced peeled potato

1 cup parsley leaves

1/2 teaspoon dry mustard

1/2 teaspoon freshly ground black pepper

1 cup 2% milk

1/4 cup snipped fresh dill

• Warm the oil in a 6-quart pot over medium-high heat for 1 minute. Add the chopped onion and sauté until transparent. Stir in the broth, cucumber, potato, parsley, and mustard. Cover the pot, and bring the mixture to a boil. Reduce the heat, and simmer until the potatoes are tender, about 15 minutes. Remove from the heat, and let cool for 10 minutes.

• Transfer the mixture to a blender jar. Process until puréed, and stir in the black pepper. Chill for 1 hour. Stir in the milk and top each serving with dill.

COOKS' TIP:

Peel the cucumber only if it is waxed.

PREP TIME: 10 MINUTES   COOK TIME: 15 MINUTES, PLUS 45 MINUTES TO CHILL

Cold Dilled Tomato Soup

MAKES 4 SERVINGS

Chill out. Dill out. And enjoy this creative, sure-to-please soup. It features tomato juice, sour cream, and sassy seasonings: red pepper flakes, onions, ginger, curry, and lemon peel.

3 cups low-sodium tomato juice

1 celery stalk, chopped

1 medium onion, chopped

1/4 teaspoon red pepper flakes

1/2 teaspoon curry powder

1/4 teaspoon ginger

1 teaspoon grated lemon peel

1 cup nonfat sour cream

2 tablespoons snipped fresh dill or chives

- In a 3-quart pot, bring 1 cup tomato juice to a boil. Add the celery, onion, and pepper flakes, and simmer for 10 minutes. Remove from the heat. Stir in the curry, ginger, lemon peel, and remaining 2 cups of tomato juice. Transfer the mixture to a blender and purée. Chill for 45 minutes.

- Stir in the sour cream. Top each serving with dill.

Chilled Carrot-Orange Soup

MAKES 8 TO 10 SERVINGS

3 tablespoons butter

1/2 teaspoon grated ginger

8 medium carrots, peeled and sliced paper-thin

1/2 cup sliced leeks (white part only)

4 cups vegetable stock or unsweetened apple juice

2 cups unsweetened orange juice

salt and pepper to taste

1 large orange, halved and sliced crosswise

10 sprigs of mint

● Melt the butter in a 6-quart pot, and sauté the ginger, carrots, and leeks until the leeks are tender. Stir in 3 cups of the stock, bring to a boil, and then reduce to a simmer. Cover lightly, and cook for about 20 minutes, or until the carrots are tender. Remove from heat and cool.

● In the container of a blender or food processor, purée the carrot mixture, in batches, until smooth. Return to the pot.

● Add the remaining stock and half the orange juice. Bring to a boil. Reduce to a simmer, and add the remaining orange juice, 1 tablespoon at a time, stirring well after each addition until the consistency is thin.

● Turn off the heat, and add salt and pepper to taste. Chill in the refrigerator for at least 2 hours.

● When ready, using a wire whisk, vigorously beat the soup before ladling into chilled soup bowls. Garnish with orange slices and mint sprigs, and serve immediately.

Chilled Guacamole Soup

MAKES 4 SERVINGS

Holy guacamole! This is a subtly delightful soup. Its flavors—creamy avocado and sour cream—are mild and pleasing. Its color—pale green—is quiet and soothing. And it all comes together with the pulse of a blender.

2 cans (14 ounces each) fat-free chicken broth

1 Florida avocado, cut into 1/2-inch cubes

1 cup nonfat sour cream

1 medium onion, chopped

2 tablespoons lemon juice

2 cloves garlic, crushed

1/2 teaspoon chili powder

1 teaspoon paprika, for garnish

• Combine the broth, avocado, sour cream, onion, lemon juice, garlic, and chili powder in a blender jar. Process until puréed. Chill for 45 minutes. Top each serving with the paprika.

COOKS' TIP:

Is your supermarket fresh out of Florida avocados? Then substitute a California variety. Just be aware that ounce for ounce, the California fruit has more than twice the fat of the Florida kind.

PREP TIME: 10 MINUTES, PLUS 30 MINUTES TO CHILL   COOK TIME: 2 HOURS TO CHILL

Chilled Cucumber Soup

MAKES 6 SERVINGS

1 large (about 12-ounce) cucumber, peeled and seeded

1 tablespoon granulated sugar

1 teaspoon salt

1 cup unflavored yogurt

1 cup tomato juice

1/2 teaspoon minced garlic

2 cups vegetable stock

1/4 cup chopped fresh mint leaves (loosely packed)

1 cup light cream

dash hot sauce

salt and pepper to taste

mint sprigs for garnish

- Place the cucumbers in a bowl, sprinkle with sugar and salt, and refrigerate for at least 30 minutes.

- In the container of a blender, combine the yogurt, tomato juice, garlic, stock, and mint leaves. Process on low until smooth. Cover and refrigerate for about 30 minutes.

- When the cucumbers are ready, rinse under cold running water and press dry between double layers of paper towels.

- Pour the yogurt mixture into a serving bowl; add the cucumbers, cream, hot sauce, and salt and pepper to taste. Cover tightly, and refrigerate for at least 2 hours before serving in well-chilled bowls, with mint sprigs as a garnish.

COOKS' TIP:

Cucumbers should always be served cold.

PREP TIME: 15 MINUTES   COOK TIME: 30 MINUTES TO CHILL

Fast Gazpacho

MAKES 4 SERVINGS

Hailing from Spain, gazpacho is an intriguing chilled soup of tomatoes, cucumbers, and other summertime vegetables. This version, which gets its zest from garlic and dried chili, is ready with the whirl of a blender's blade.

2 cans (15 ounces each) diced tomatoes

1 1/2 cups reduced-sodium tomato juice

1 medium cucumber, chopped

1 green sweet pepper, chopped

1 medium onion, chopped

1 mild dried chili pepper, seeded and chopped

4 cloves garlic, chopped

2 teaspoons red wine vinegar

2 teaspoons olive oil

2 cups croutons, for garnish

• Combine the tomatoes, tomato juice, cucumber, sweet pepper, onion, chili pepper, garlic, vinegar, and olive oil in a blender. Process the mixture until the vegetables are partially puréed. Chill the soup until cold, 30 minutes. Top each serving with croutons.

COOKS' TIPS:

• Ancho peppers, which are dried poblano peppers, give this recipe just the right zip. If you can't find them, simply use 1/4 to 1/2 of a minced, seeded cayenne pepper.

• Peel the cucumber only if it is waxed.

7/12/08 — Good Quick + Easy. used 1/2 of jalapeno pepper.

PREP TIME: 5 MINUTES   COOK TIME: 15 MINUTES, PLUS 2 HOURS TO CHILL

Sweet & Spicy Carrot Soup

MAKES 6 TO 8 SERVINGS

1 1/2 cups cold water

1/4 teaspoon salt

16-ounce package frozen carrots

1 1/2 cups orange juice

1/2 teaspoon nutmeg

1 cup vegetable stock

1 orange, sliced thin, for garnish

mint sprigs for garnish

● In a 6-quart pot, combine the water, salt, and carrots. Bring to a boil, then reduce to a simmer. Cover lightly, and cook for 8 to 10 minutes, or until the carrots are very tender.

● In the container of a blender, purée the carrots and cooking liquid until smooth.

● In a large bowl, combine the puréed carrots with the orange juice, nutmeg, and stock, blending well. Cover the bowl and refrigerate 2 hours or until well chilled. Serve cold with a garnish of a fresh orange slice and a mint sprig in each bowl.

PREP TIME: 10 MINUTES   COOK TIME: 50 MINUTES, PLUS 4 HOURS TO CHILL

Chilled Tomato Basil Soup

MAKES 4 SERVINGS

3 tablespoons butter

1 tablespoon vegetable oil

1 medium yellow onion, finely chopped

1 medium leek (white part only), finely chopped

1 medium carrot, peeled and finely chopped

1 medium celery stalk, finely chopped

2 tablespoons chopped fresh basil

2 cans (16 ounces each) diced tomatoes

3 tablespoons tomato paste

2 tablespoons all-purpose flour

2 1/2 cups vegetable stock

1/2 cup light cream

salt and pepper to taste

fresh basil leaves for garnish

1/4 cup sour cream or unflavored yogurt for garnish

COOKS' TIP:

Keep basil growing in your kitchen; it often comes in handy.

• Heat the butter and oil together in a medium saucepan, and sauté the onion, leek, carrot, celery, and chopped basil until the onion is transparent. Add the tomatoes and tomato paste, and cook, stirring occasionally, for about 5 minutes. Stir in the flour until incorporated, and add the stock. Bring to a boil, then reduce to a simmer. Cover lightly, and cook without stirring for about 20 minutes. Remove from heat.

• In the container of a blender or food processor, purée the mixture in batches, until smooth. Strain and press through a fine sieve, and return the mixture to the pot. Bring to a boil, then reduce to a simmer, and cook for 3 to 4 minutes.

• Turn off the heat, stir in the cream, and add salt and pepper to taste. Cool slightly. Cover tightly and refrigerate for at least 4 hours.

• Using a wire whisk, stir the soup vigorously. Ladle into chilled bowls, and serve with a garnish of basil leaves and a dollop of sour cream.

Avocado & Spinach Soup

MAKES 4 SERVINGS

This soup is quick and easy to prepare but needs a couple of hours to chill.

2 tablespoons butter
1 package (16 ounces) frozen chopped spinach, thawed
3 tablespoons all-purpose flour
2 cups soy milk
1 1/2 cups vegetable stock
pinch of nutmeg
2 large avocados, finely chopped
1 cup farmers' or cottage cheese
salt and pepper to taste
1 small avocado, sliced and halved, for garnish

● Melt the butter in a saucepan and sauté the spinach over low heat, stirring frequently for 7 to 10 minutes. Sprinkle in the flour, and cook, stirring constantly, for about 1 minute, before adding the soy milk and stock. Bring to a boil, and add the nutmeg. Reduce to a simmer, and add the chopped avocados and cheese. Remove from heat, and in the container of a blender or food processor, purée the soup in batches, until smooth. Transfer to a bowl, cover tightly, and refrigerate for 2 hours.

● When ready, add salt and pepper to taste. Ladle into chilled soup bowls. Garnish with sliced avocado.

Chilled Red Pepper Soup

MAKES 6 SERVINGS

1 tablespoon butter
3 large red bell peppers, stemmed, seeded, and finely diced
1 medium yellow onion, chopped
1 medium clove garlic, minced
1 cup vegetable stock
1/2 teaspoon crushed dried thyme
hot pepper sauce to taste
1 cup half-and-half
salt and pepper to taste

● Melt the butter in a saucepan and sauté the peppers, onion, and garlic until the onion is translucent. Add the stock, thyme, and pepper sauce to taste. Bring to a boil, then reduce to a simmer, cover lightly, and cook for about 10 minutes, or until most of the liquid has been absorbed. Remove from heat.

● In the container of a blender or food processor, purée the mixture until smooth. Pour into a large bowl, and using a wire whisk, vigorously beat in the half-and-half. Cover and refrigerate for at least 4 hours.

● When ready, using the wire whisk, vigorously beat the soup, add salt and pepper to taste, and ladle into chilled bowls. Serve immediately.

PREP TIME: 15 MINUTES   COOK TIME: 50 MINUTES, PLUS 1 HOUR 10 MINUTES TO CHILL

Chilled Cream-of-Vegetable Soup

MAKES 6 SERVINGS

3 *parsley sprigs*

1 *bay leaf*

1/2 *teaspoon crushed dried thyme*

2 *whole cloves*

1 *small clove garlic, crushed*

1 *cup chopped celery leaves*

1 *medium carrot, trimmed and diced*

1 *small green bell pepper, stemmed, seeded, and diced*

1 *cup finely chopped spinach leaves*

1 *large white onion, chopped*

4 *cups vegetable stock*

1/4 *cup rice*

2 *egg yolks*

2 *cups half-and-half*

salt and pepper to taste

sour cream for garnish

minced parsley for garnish

minced chives for garnish

2 *medium tomatoes, peeled and chopped, for garnish*

● Tie the parsley, bay leaf, thyme, cloves, and garlic in a square of cheesecloth to make a spice bag.

● In a 6-quart pot, combine the celery leaves, carrot, green pepper, spinach, onion, stock, spice bag, and rice. Bring to a boil. Reduce to a simmer, cover lightly, and cook, stirring occasionally, for about 30 minutes, or until the rice is tender. Discard herbs in the cheesecloth, and remove from heat.

● In the container of a blender or food processor, purée the mixture in batches, processing until smooth. Return to the pot, and reheat.

● In a small bowl, whisk together the egg yolks and several tablespoons of soup until smooth. Stir this mixture back into the hot soup mix until incorporated. (Do not allow to boil.) Add the half-and-half, heat through, remove from heat, and add salt and pepper to taste. Cool to room temperature. Chill in the refrigerator for about 1 hour.

● When ready to serve, whisk the soup vigorously and ladle into chilled soup bowls. Serve immediately with sour cream, minced parsley, chives, and tomatoes.

PREP TIME: 10 MINUTES   COOK TIME: 2 HOURS TO CHILL

African Tomato & Avocado Soup

MAKES 2 TO 4 SERVINGS

1 large avocado

1 tablespoon fresh lemon juice

3 cans (16 ounces each) crushed tomatoes

2 tablespoons tomato paste

1 cup buttermilk or sour milk

1 tablespoon safflower or olive oil

2 tablespoons finely minced fresh parsley

salt and pepper to taste

hot pepper sauce to taste

1 cucumber, peeled, seeded, and diced, for garnish

whipped sour cream, unflavored yogurt, or crème fraîche, for garnish

● Mash the avocado with the lemon juice.

● In a blender or food processor, combine the tomatoes, tomato paste, buttermilk, and oil. Process on high until smooth. Pour into a bowl, add the avocado mixture, parsley, seasonings, and pepper sauce to taste.

● Refrigerate for at least 2 hours before serving. When ready, serve with cucumbers as a garnish and sour cream on the side.

PREP TIME: 10 MINUTES

Arugula Soup with Tomato Salsa

MAKES 4 TO 6 SERVINGS

2 large ripe avocados, chopped

1 small bunch arugula leaves

3 tablespoons fresh lemon juice

1 small clove garlic, chopped

1/4 cup light cream

1 cup ice cubes

1 tablespoon grated gingerroot

salt and pepper to taste

5 tablespoons tomato salsa

water as desired

● In a medium bowl, combine all the ingredients, except the water, and purée in batches using a food processor or blender. Stir in enough water to reach desired consistency.

● Spoon into chilled bowls, and serve immediately with bruschetta and whole cloves of garlic, cut in half, on the side.

COOKS' TIP:

Arugula is available in specialty produce markets and sold in small bunches with roots still attached.

PREP TIME: 10 MINUTES COOK TIME: 15 MINUTES, PLUS 4 HOURS TO CHILL

Curried Apple & Carrot Soup

MAKES ABOUT 3 CUPS

1¼ cups unsweetened apple juice

1 medium McIntosh apple, pared and chopped

1 cup cooked sliced carrots (about 2 medium carrots)

¼ cup shredded Gouda cheese

3 ounces cream cheese

1 tablespoon honey

2 teaspoons lime juice or lemon juice

½ teaspoon curry powder

½ cup chopped toasted walnuts for garnish

COOKS' TIP:

This is a sweet soup with just enough of a bite to make your guests come back for a second taste.

● In a saucepan, combine the apple juice, apple, and carrots. Bring to a boil, and stir in the Gouda cheese. Cook, stirring constantly, until the cheese has melted. Remove from heat.

● In the container of a blender, purée the cheese mixture, in batches, until smooth. Pour half the mixture back into the blender, and add the cream cheese, honey, lime juice, and curry powder. Process on high until smooth. Pour all of the mixture into a bowl, cover tightly, and chill for at least 4 hours.

● When ready, serve in chilled bowls topped with nuts.

PREP TIME: 15 MINUTES   COOK TIME: 40 MINUTES, PLUS 4 HOURS TO CHILL

Chilled Pea Pod Soup

MAKES 6 TO 8 SERVINGS

2 pounds fresh green pea pods
1/2 cup butter
8 scallions, sliced
2 quarts vegetable stock
2 tablespoons fresh tarragon leaves
16 leaves romaine lettuce
1/2 cup crème fraîche
salt and pepper to taste
granulated sugar to taste
chopped fresh pea pods for garnish

COOKS' TIP:

As vegetables go, the pea pod is considered sweet; be very careful when you add the sugar.

● Under running water, snap the ends off the pea pods and remove the strings.

● Melt the butter in a 6-quart pot, and sauté the pods and scallions together, stirring frequently, until the scallions are tender. Stir in the stock and tarragon, bring to a boil; reduce to a simmer, cover lightly, and cook, stirring occasionally, for about 15 minutes. Add the romaine and continue to cook for about 5 minutes, or until the lettuce is completely wilted. Remove from heat.

● In the container of a blender or food processor, purée the soup, in batches, until smooth. Strain through a fine sieve into a large bowl. Stir in the crème fraîche, cover, and chill in the refrigerator for at least 4 hours.

● When ready to serve, vigorously wisk the soup, and add salt and pepper to taste. Stir in the sugar. Ladle into chilled bowls, and garnish with chopped pea pods.

PREP TIME: 10 MINUTES   COOK TIME: 45 MINUTES, PLUS 20 MINUTES TO COOL

Asparagus & Vegetable Soup

MAKES 4 TO 6 SERVINGS

1/4 cup butter

11/2 pounds fresh asparagus, tips and stalks
  separated

1 cup chopped leeks (white part only)

1/2 cup chopped yellow onion

1/2 cup chopped celery

1 small baking potato, peeled and diced

31/2 cups vegetable stock

1 teaspoon fresh lemon juice

1/2 cup half-and-half

salt and pepper to taste

paprika to taste (optional)

whipped cream for garnish

● Melt the butter in a skillet, and sauté the asparagus tips (reserve the stalks), leeks, onion, celery, and potato until heated through. Cover lightly, cooking over a low heat until the potatoes are soft, about 20 minutes.

● In a 6-quart pot, combine the stock and remaining asparagus stalks (without tips). Bring to a boil. Reduce to a simmer, cover lightly, and cook for about 10 minutes. Remove from heat, and strain through a fine sieve. Discard the stalks and return the liquid to the pot.

● In the container of a blender or food processor, purée the vegetables from the skillet until smooth. Stir the purée into the stock, and add the lemon juice, half-and-half, and salt and pepper to taste. Cool to room temperature and refrigerate.

● When ready to serve, using a wire whisk, beat until smooth. Serve cold, sprinkled with paprika and with whipped cream.

Cool Fruit Soups

Spiced Mixed Fruit Soup •

Apple Raisin Soup •

Cold Papaya Soup •

Red, White & Blue Soup •

Chilled Curried Peach Soup •

Chilled Blueberry Soup •

Colorful Strawberry Soup •
with Kiwi

Chilled Raspberry Soup •

• Chilled Raspberry Orange Soup

• Orange-Mango Soup

• Currant & Cranberry Soup

• Chilled Cranberry Soup

• White Grape Gazpacho

• Chilled Cantaloupe Soup

• White Peach Soup

• Classic Strawberry Soup

• Cinnamon Peach Soup

PREP TIME: 10 MINUTES   COOK TIME: 15 MINUTES, PLUS 30 MINUTES TO CHILL

Spiced Mixed Fruit Soup

MAKES 4 SERVINGS

Apple juice and spice and everything nice—pears, watermelon, grapes, and nectarines—that's what this heavenly soup is made of.

2 cups apple juice

1 cinnamon stick

2 whole allspice berries

2 lemon tea bags

2 cups vanilla low-fat yogurt

1 Bartlett pear, cored and chopped

1 cup cubed watermelon

1 cup white grapes

1 cup red grapes

1 nectarine, pitted and chopped

● Combine the apple juice, cinnamon, allspice, and tea bags in a 2-quart saucepan. Cover the pot, and bring the mixture to a boil. Reduce the heat, and simmer for 5 minutes. Discard the cinnamon, allspice, and tea. Chill for 30 minutes.

● In a serving bowl, whisk together the yogurt and 1 1/2 to 2 cups of the juice mixture. Determine how much juice mixture to use by the consistency of the soup. Stir in the pears, watermelon, white grapes, red grapes, and nectarine.

COOKS' TIPS:

• Use a slotted spoon to fish out the cinnamon, allspice, and tea bags.
• For bright, fresh-looking pears and nectarines, cut them right before serving. When exposed to air, the flesh of these fruits oxidizes and turns brown.

PREP TIME: 5 MINUTES   COOK TIME: 25 MINUTES,
PLUS 20 MINUTES TO CHILL

Apple Raisin Soup

MAKES 3 TO 4 SERVINGS

Apples and raisins are a tried-and-true pairing. They've been used in everything from cookies to bread to poultry stuffing—they're a natural for soup.

2 cups unsweetened apple juice or cider
2 large McIntosh apples, pared and diced
3/4 cup seedless raisins
2-inch cinnamon stick
1 tablespoon packed light brown sugar
1 tablespoon brandy or rum

• In a large pot or Dutch oven, combine the apple juice, apples, raisins, and cinnamon. Bring to a boil, then reduce heat, cover, and simmer for about 15 minutes, or until the apples are fork tender.

• Remove from heat, stir in the brown sugar and brandy, cover tightly, and chill until ready to serve. When ready, discard the cinnamon stick, and serve as desired.

COOKS' TIP:

Most supermarkets carry a nonalcoholic brandy or rum flavoring next to the vanilla extract.

PREP TIME: 10 MINUTES   COOK TIME: 4 HOURS TO CHILL

Cold Papaya Soup

MAKES 2 SERVINGS

1 medium (6-inch) ripe papaya
sugar to taste
2 tablespoons fresh lime juice
water or unsweetened apple juice

• Peel and seed the papaya; cut the flesh into chunks. Reserve the seeds in the refrigerator.

• In a blender or food processor, purée the papaya until very smooth. Pour into a bowl, and sweeten with sugar to taste. Stir in the lime juice. If the mixture is too thick, add water or apple juice, 1 teaspoon at a time. The soup should be very thick.

• Cover and chill in the refrigerator for at least 4 hours. Serve in chilled fruit cups with a small spoonful of the reserved seeds in the center.

Red, White & Blue Soup

MAKES 4 SERVINGS

Refreshingly tart flavors. Smooth, creamy texture. Vibrant red, white, and blue colors. All make this soup of blueberries, raspberries, and lemon yogurt a dinner winner.

2 cups blueberries

2 tablespoons honey

1/2 cup white grape juice

1 1/4 cups buttermilk

1 cup red raspberries plus more for garnish

1/2 cup vanilla low-fat yogurt

1 teaspoon grated lemon peel

- Combine the blueberries, honey, and 1/4 cup grape juice in a microwave-safe bowl. Microwave on High for 3 minutes. Transfer the blueberry mixture to a blender, and add 3/4 cup buttermilk. Purée the mixture, and transfer it to a medium-size bowl. Chill for 1 hour.

- Combine the raspberries and remaining 1/4 cup grape juice in a microwave-safe bowl. Microwave on High for 2 minutes. Transfer the raspberry mixture to a clean blender. Purée the mixture, and transfer it to a small bowl. Chill for 1 hour.

- Whisk together the yogurt and lemon peel.

- Just before serving, whisk the remaining 1/2 cup buttermilk into the blueberry mixture. Divide the mixture among 4 serving bowls. Swirl some of the raspberry purée into each bowl of soup. Top each serving with a dollop of yogurt and raspberries.

PREP TIME: 10 MINUTES   COOK TIME: 25 MINUTES, PLUS 1 HOUR TO CHILL

Chilled Curried Peach Soup

MAKES ABOUT 1 QUART

1 1/2 *cups diced fresh peaches*
2 *cups vegetable stock or unsweetened apple juice*
2 *tablespoons butter*
1 *small yellow onion, chopped*
1/2 *teaspoon curry powder*
pinch turmeric
1 *small bay leaf*
2 *tablespoons all-purpose flour*
salt and pepper to taste
peach-flavored yogurt for garnish

• In a blender or food processor, purée the peaches and stock until smooth.

• Melt the butter in a 6-quart pot, and sauté the onion until tender. Add the curry powder, turmeric, and bay leaf. Cook, stirring constantly, for about 2 minutes.

• Turn off the heat, sprinkle in the flour, and stir until incorporated and smooth.

• Return to the heat. Pouring in a narrow stream and stirring constantly, blend in the peach purée. Bring to a boil, then reduce to a simmer, and cook for about 3 minutes.

• Turn off the heat, discard the bay leaf, and add salt and pepper to taste. Cool slightly before chilling in the refrigerator for at least 1 hour.

• When ready, using a wire whisk, vigorously beat the soup; ladle into chilled bowls. Serve immediately with the peach-flavored yogurt on the side.

PREP TIME: 10 MINUTES   COOK TIME: 1 HOUR TO CHILL

Chilled Blueberry Soup

MAKES 4 SERVINGS

1 pint fresh blueberries

1 cup fresh unsweetened orange juice

1/2 cup sour cream

1 tablespoon granulated sugar

1 tablespoon packed light brown sugar

1/4 teaspoon ground nutmeg

1 tablespoon sour cream for garnish

● In a blender or food processor, purée blueberries, orange juice, 1/2 cup sour cream, granulated sugar, brown sugar, and nutmeg until smooth. Pour into a large bowl, cover, and chill for at least an hour.

● In a small bowl, using a wire whisk, beat the remaining sour cream until smooth. Spoon into a pastry bag fitted with a fine round tip.

● Pour the soup into chilled bowls, and squeeze the sour cream from the pastry bag onto the top of the soup in a design.

PREP TIME: 20 MINUTES   COOK TIME: 45 MINUTES TO CHILL

Colorful Strawberry
Soup with Kiwi

MAKES 4 SERVINGS

Create a stir with this creamy soup, which is plump with strawberries, peaches, and kiwifruit. It's sweet. It's fruity. It's pretty. And it's a hit with the young and young-at-heart.

1 pint (about 12 ounces) strawberries, sliced
¼ cup white grape juice
2 tablespoons honey
2 cups vanilla low-fat yogurt
2 peaches, peeled and chopped
1 kiwifruit, peeled and thinly sliced, for garnish
8 fresh mint leaves for garnish

● Set 1 cup strawberries aside. Combine the grape juice, honey, and remaining strawberries in a microwave-safe bowl. Microwave on High for 3 minutes; let cool for 10 minutes.

● Transfer the strawberry juice mixture to a blender and add the yogurt. Process until puréed. Transfer to a bowl, and chill the mixture for 45 minutes.

● Stir the peaches and reserved strawberries into the soup. Top each serving with the kiwi and mint.

COOKS' TIP:

For fresh-looking peaches, cut them right before stirring them into the soup.

PREP TIME: 5 MINUTES   COOK TIME: 25 MINUTES, PLUS 8 HOURS TO CHILL

Chilled Raspberry Soup

MAKES ABOUT 4 SERVINGS

2 packages (10 ounces each) frozen raspberries,
   thawed

2 cups burgundy wine

2 1/2 cups water

3-inch stick cinnamon

2 teaspoons cornstarch or arrowroot

2 tablespoons water

1 cup heavy cream blended with 2 tablespoons
   powdered sugar

• In a 6-quart pot, combine the raspberries, wine, water, and cinnamon. Bring to a boil. Then reduce to a simmer, cover lightly, and cook, stirring occasionally, for about 15 minutes. Remove from heat.

• In the container of a blender or food processor, purée the soup in batches until smooth. Strain through a sieve, discarding any seeds, and return the mixture to the pot.

• Dissolve the cornstarch in the water. Stir the cornstarch mixture into the soup and return to a boil. Cook, stirring frequently, for 2 to 3 minutes or until barely thickened. Remove from heat, cool a little, cover tightly, and refrigerate for at least 8 hours.

• When ready to serve, ladle into chilled bowls, and drizzle on the cream. Using a knife, make several swirls in the soup, and serve immediately.

PREP TIME: 15 MINUTES   COOK TIME: 8 HOURS TO CHILL

Chilled Raspberry Orange Soup

MAKES ABOUT 12 SERVINGS

1¹/2 tablespoons unflavored gelatin

¹/3 cup cold water

³/4 cup hot water

3 packages (10 ounces each) frozen raspberries,
   thawed

3¹/2 cups sour cream

1¹/3 cups orange juice

1¹/3 cups half-and-half

1¹/3 cups white port wine

¹/3 cup grenadine or sweet red wine

2 tablespoons crème de noyaux liqueur

salt and white pepper to taste

mint for garnish

whole raspberries for garnish

● In a saucepan, soak the gelatin in the cold water for about 5 minutes. Add the hot water and heat, stirring until the gelatin is dissolved.

● In the container of a blender or food processor, purée the raspberries until smooth. Press through a fine sieve into a large bowl.

● In the same bowl, add the sour cream, orange juice, half-and-half, port, grenadine, and crème de noyaux. Using a wire whisk, vigorously beat until smooth.

● Cover and chill in the refrigerator for at least 8 hours or overnight. When ready, whisk the soup, add the salt and pepper to taste, and ladle into chilled bowls. Garnish with gelatin, mint, and raspberries, and serve immediately.

PREP TIME: 10 MINUTES, PLUS 1 HOUR TO CHILL   COOK TIME: 2 DAYS TO CHILL

Orange-Mango Soup

MAKES ABOUT 4 SERVINGS

1 tablespoon orange zest
3 large very ripe mangoes, pared
1 1/2 cups buttermilk
1 1/2 cups fresh orange juice
3 teaspoons honey, or to taste, warmed
1 tablespoon lemon or lime juice
4 slices orange for garnish
8 small fresh mint leaves for garnish

- In the container of a blender or food processor, purée the orange zest and mangoes until smooth. Strain through a fine sieve, pressing with the back of a spoon. Pour the mixture into a bowl, cover tightly, and refrigerate for at least 1 hour.

- When the mixture is chilled, stir in the buttermilk, orange juice, and 2 teaspoons honey. (If it appears too thick, add more buttermilk.)

- Cover tightly and refrigerate for about 2 days.

- When ready, add the lemon juice and remaining 1 teaspoon honey. Pour into chilled bowls. Float a slice of orange on top, garnish of mint leaves, and serve immediately.

PREP TIME: 5 MINUTES   COOK TIME: 25 MINUTES, PLUS 2 HOURS TO CHILL

Currant & Cranberry Soup

MAKES 4 TO 6 SERVINGS

Red currants and black currants are wonderful when cooked and blended with cranberries.

6 ounces fresh red currants

6 ounces fresh black currants

6 ounces fresh cranberries

1 1/2 cups dry white wine

1/2 cup granulated sugar

2-inch cinnamon stick

1 tablespoon grated orange zest

juice of 1 orange

1 1/2 cups water

1 tablespoon crème de cassis liqueur (optional)

2/3 cup sour cream (optional)

black currant leaves for garnish

- In a 6-quart pot, combine the red and the black currants, cranberries, wine, sugar, cinnamon, orange zest, juice, and water. Bring to a boil, and reduce to a simmer. Cook, stirring occasionally, for about 15 minutes, or until the fruit is tender.

- Remove from heat. Discard the cinnamon stick.

- In the container of a blender or food processor, purée the mixture, in batches, until smooth. Press through a fine sieve to remove the seeds. Pour into a bowl, cover tightly, and refrigerate for at least 2 hours.

- When ready to serve, using a wire whisk, beat in the crème de cassis until light, and ladle into chilled bowls. Daub a spoonful of sour cream on the top, swirl, and garnish with black currant leaves.

COOKS' TIP:

Try a tasty alternative to plain sour cream—Amaretto-flavored sour cream. Beat 2 2/3 cup sour cream and 1 tablespoon amaretto vigorously together. Chill until needed.

PREP TIME: 5 MINUTES   COOK TIME: 25 MINUTES, PLUS 30 MINUTES TO CHILL

Chilled Cranberry Soup

MAKES 4 SERVINGS

1 tablespoon cornstarch

2 tablespoons cold water

1 package (12 ounces) fresh cranberries

3 cups water

1 cup granulated sugar

3/4 cup packed light brown sugar

2 cinnamon sticks

2 allspice berries

2 whole cloves

4 black peppercorns

3/4 cup heavy cream, whipped to soft peaks

1/2 cup dry red wine or to taste

COOKS' TIP:

This would be great served at Thanksgiving.

• In a cup, blend the cornstarch and cold water. Set aside.

• Thoroughly rinse the cranberries under running water, shaking to remove excess water.

• In a 6-quart pot, combine the 3 cups of water, two sugars, cinnamon, allspice, cloves, and peppercorns. Bring to a boil. Reduce to a simmer, add the cranberries, and cook, stirring occasionally, for about 15 minutes, or until the berries are tender.

• Stir in the cornstarch mixture, bring to a boil, and cook, stirring constantly, until thickened.

• Turn off the heat, chill slightly, and refrigerate until ready to serve.

• When ready, stir in the whipped cream and wine, adjust the flavor for sweetness, and serve in well-chilled bowls.

PREP TIME: 25 MINUTES   COOK TIME: 5 MINUTES, PLUS 8 HOURS TO CHILL

White Grape Gazpacho

MAKES ABOUT 6 SERVINGS

1/4 cup blanched almonds

2 cloves garlic, peeled

salt and pepper to taste

4 slices stale white bread, crusts removed

4 cups ice water

7 tablespoons canola oil

3 tablespoons white wine vinegar

2 tablespoons sherry wine vinegar

1 tablespoon butter or margarine

1 clove garlic, crushed

6 slices white bread, crusts removed, cubed

1 1/2 cups seedless green grapes

COOKS' TIP:

Try freezing any fruit you plan to use as a garnish while you are chilling the soup in the refrigerator. This is a great way to keep a chilled soup cool during the meal.

- In a blender, combine the almonds, 2 cloves garlic, and salt and pepper to taste. Process on high until smooth.

- Place 4 slices of bread in a bowl, and add 1 cup ice water. Soak through, squeeze out the water, and put the bread in the blender with the garlic mixture.

- With the processor running on low, add 6 tablespoons of the canola oil, and 1 cup ice water. Add the vinegars and blend on high speed until smooth. Add 1 cup of water, and process on high for about 1 minute. Pour into a bowl, and add the remaining 1 cup of water. Add salt and pepper to taste, cover tightly, and refrigerate for at least 8 hours.

- When ready, prepare the croutons in a skillet. Heat the butter, remaining oil, and crushed garlic. Cook, stirring constantly, for about 2 minutes. Add the bread cubes and cook, tossing, until toasted.

- Ladle the cold soup into chilled bowls, and sprinkle the croutons and green grapes on top. Serve immediately.

PREP TIME: 5 MINUTES   COOK TIME: 10 MINUTES, PLUS 2 HOURS TO CHILL

Chilled Cantaloupe Soup

MAKES 6 SERVINGS

1 large ripe cantaloupe, cubed
orange juice to cover
2 tablespoons fresh lemon juice
pinch of ground cinnamon
pinch of curry powder
pinch of turmeric powder
fresh mint leaves for garnish

- Put the cantaloupe and orange juice in a large saucepan, bring to a boil, and immediately remove from heat; cool slightly.

- In the container of a blender or food processor, purée the cantaloupe mixture until smooth. Add the lemon juice, cinnamon, curry powder, and turmeric. Pour into a bowl, and chill in the refrigerator for at least 2 hours. Serve in chilled bowls with a mint leaf garnish on top.

COOKS' TIP:

The spices give the cantaloupe a nice flare, but remember that too much of the curry can make this soup sour.

White Peach Soup

MAKES 6 SERVINGS

White peaches, with their strip of brilliant red flesh, give this slightly sweet soup a soft pink tint. Red plums and green mint provide flavorful, colorful accents. It's a wonderful dish to serve for a cool lunch or a dessert.

4 medium white peaches, peeled and pitted

2 cups vanilla low-fat yogurt

1/4 teaspoon cinnamon

1 teaspoon honey

2 red plums, pitted and coarsely chopped

*1 teaspoon snipped fresh mint or 1/4 teaspoon
  dried mint leaves*

● Combine the peaches, yogurt, cinnamon, and honey in a food processor. Process the mixture until it is smooth, about 30 seconds. Transfer the mixture to a serving bowl. Stir in the plums, and chill the soup for 30 minutes. Top each serving with the mint.

COOKS' TIPS:

● Can't find any white peaches? Then use the standard yellow variety; just be aware that the soup's color will be a soft peach, not pink.
● Variation: You may subsitute nectarines for the peaches and another variety of plums for the red plums.

PREP TIME: 10 MINUTES   COOK TIME: 15 MINUTES, PLUS 2 HOURS TO CHILL

Classic
Strawberry Soup

MAKES 6 SERVINGS

Strawberry soup is an old standard and thought to be one of the first cold berry soups created.

1/2 teaspoon instant tapioca

1 cup fresh unsweetened orange juice

2 pints fresh strawberries

1 tablespoon fresh lemon juice

cinnamon to taste

allspice to taste

1/2 cup granulated sugar

1 teaspoon lemon zest

1 cup buttermilk

1 thinly sliced lime for garnish

additional sliced strawberries for garnish

• In a bowl, combine the tapioca and orange juice, and set aside for about 5 minutes. In the container of a blender or food processor, purée the strawberries until smooth.

• In a saucepan, combine the strawberry purée and tapioca mixture. Stir in lemon juice, cinnamon, and allspice to taste. Bring to a boil, reduce to a simmer, and cook, stirring constantly, until thickened.

• Turn off the heat. Stir in the sugar. Cool slightly, cover tightly, and refrigerate for about 2 hours, or until completely chilled.

• To serve, stir in the lemon zest and buttermilk. Using a wire whisk, stir vigorously before adjusting the sweetness to taste. Ladle into well-chilled bowls, garnish as desired, and serve immediately.

PREP TIME: 5 MINUTES   COOK TIME: 15 MINUTES, PLUS 4 HOURS TO CHILL

Cinnamon Peach Soup

MAKES 4 TO 6 SERVINGS

The blend of cinnamon and good, ripe peaches is heavenly.

3 *whole cloves*
3 *allspice berries*
3 *cardamom pods*
2 *pounds ripe peaches, peeled and diced*
2 *cups fresh orange juice*
3 *tablespoons fresh lime juice*
3 *to 4 tablespoons warmed honey*
1 *teaspoon ground cinnamon*
1 *teaspoon ground ginger*
1 *cup unflavored yogurt or sour cream*
1 *tablespoon diced candied ginger*
salt and pepper
sprigs of fresh mint for garnish

- Tie up the cloves, allspice, and cardamom in a 4-inch square of cheesecloth.

- In a large pot or Dutch oven, combine the peaches, spice bag, orange juice, lime juice, honey, cinnamon, and ginger. Simmer for 5 to 10 minutes, or until the fruit is well softened.

- Remove from heat, discard the spice bundle, and cool the soup slightly.

- In the container of a blender or food processor, purée the soup in batches until smooth. Place in a bowl, cover tightly, and chill for at least 4 hours.

- Just before serving, using a wire whisk, beat in the yogurt and stir in the ginger. Add salt and pepper to taste, garnish with mint sprigs, and serve immediately.

Hearty Chowders

PREP TIME: 5 MINUTES   COOK TIME: 25 MINUTES

Butternut Chowder
with Smoked Salmon

MAKES 4 SERVINGS

This soup is everything a chowder should be: thick, creamy, chunky, and flavorful.

1 pound butternut squash, peeled and cut
    into 1/2-inch cubes
1 can (14 ounces) reduced-sodium vegetable broth
1 large white onion, chopped
1/2 teaspoon dried rosemary
1/4 teaspoon white pepper
1 can (15 ounces) cream-style corn
1 cup frozen corn
8 ounces smoked salmon bits
1/2 cup 2% milk

● Combine the squash, broth, onion, rosemary, and pepper in a 6-quart pot. Cover the pot, and bring the mixture to a boil. Reduce the heat, and simmer until the squash is tender, 12 to 15 minutes. Using a potato masher, mash the squash until the mixture is smooth.

● Stir in the cream-style corn, the frozen corn, and the salmon. Cover and simmer 10 minutes more. Stir in the milk.

COOKS' TIP:

For maximum rosemary flavor, crush the herb between your fingers before adding it to the chowder.

PREP TIME: 5 MINUTES   COOK TIME: 35 MINUTES

Chicken-Corn Chowder with Stuffed Olives

MAKES 4 SERVINGS

In this simple recipe, a tasty combination—chicken and corn—makes for a family-favorite chowder. Mashed potatoes thicken the broth; garlic and hot-pepper sauce impart zing.

1 teaspoon olive oil

3/4 pound chicken breast, cut into 1/2-inch cubes

1 1/2 cups chicken broth

1 large potato, peeled and cut into 1/2-inch cubes

4 cloves garlic, crushed

1 can (15 ounces) reduced-sodium cream-style corn

1 1/2 cups frozen corn

4 scallions, sliced

1/2 cup 2% milk

2 to 3 drops Louisiana hot-pepper sauce

1 tablespoon stuffed olives, chopped

● Warm the oil in a 6-quart pot over medium-high heat for 1 minute. Add the chicken and sauté until the pieces are cooked through and lightly browned, 5 to 10 minutes. Transfer to a bowl, and cover with foil to keep the chicken warm.

● Pour 1 cup of the broth into the same pot. Add the potato and garlic. Cover the pot, and bring the mixture to a boil. Reduce the heat, and simmer the mixture until the potato is tender, about 12 minutes. Using a potato masher, mash the potato mixture.

● Stir in the cream-style corn, frozen corn, scallions, milk, hot sauce, chicken, and remaining broth. Heat thoroughly, about 6 minutes. Stir in the olives and serve immediately.

COOKS' TIP:

Add hot-pepper sauce with caution, tasting the soup after each drop. Why? The firepower of hot-pepper sauces varies dramatically. Some are relatively mild; others, scorching.

6/15/06 Great - very hearty; should be called Flounder/potato soup.

Flounder-Jack Chowder

MAKES 4 SERVINGS

Taste-testers pronounced this creamy seafood and cheese chowder delicious. I think you'll agree.

2 teaspoons butter

1 large onion, chopped

2 celery stalks, chopped

2 cloves garlic

2 large potatoes, peeled and cut into 1/2-inch cubes

1 can (14 ounces) fat-free chicken broth

1 pound flounder, cut into bite-size pieces

1/2 cup skim milk

1/2 cup shredded reduced-sodium Monterey Jack cheese

1 teaspoon Louisiana-style hot-pepper sauce

2 tablespoons snipped fresh chives

- Melt butter in a 6-quart pot over medium-high heat. Add the onion, celery, and garlic, and cook until the onion is golden, about 3 minutes. Add the potatoes and broth. Cover the pot, and bring the mixture to a boil. Reduce the heat, and simmer until the potatoes and celery are tender, about 12 minutes. Using a slotted spoon, transfer 2 cups of the vegetables to a bowl; cover the bowl with foil to keep them warm.

- Using a handheld immersion blender, purée the vegetables remaining in the pot. Add the flounder. Cover the pot, and gently simmer the mixture until the fish is tender, 3 to 5 minutes. Gently stir in the milk, Monterey Jack cheese, hot-pepper sauce, and reserved vegetables. Heat the soup throughout; do not boil. Top each serving with chives.

COOKS' TIP:

Flounder is a delicate fish. To keep it from falling apart, simmer and stir the soup gently.

PREP TIME: 5 MINUTES   COOK TIME: 20 MINUTES

Easy Manhattan-Style Clam Chowder

MAKES 4 SERVINGS

Tomato clam chowder aficionados: This chunky version is brimming with clams, tomatoes, potatoes, and bacon, and is ready to serve in less than 30 minutes.

4 ounces Canadian bacon, diced
1 large Spanish onion, chopped
1 stalk celery, thinly sliced
1 can (10 ounces) clam juice
1 can (15 ounces) whole tomatoes, cut up
2 medium red potatoes, chopped
2 bay leaves
1/4 teaspoon lemon pepper
1 can (6 ounces) minced clams with juice
1/4 cup snipped fresh parsley

- Sauté the bacon in a 6-quart pot until lightly browned. Add the onion and celery, and sauté until the onion is transparent, about 3 minutes.

- Stir in the clam juice, tomatoes, potatoes, bay leaves, and lemon pepper. Cover the pot, and bring the mixture to a boil. Reduce the heat, and simmer until the potatoes are tender, 12 to 15 minutes.

- Stir in the clams and simmer the soup for 5 minutes more. Discard the bay leaves. Top each serving with the parsley.

COOKS' TIP:

If you use fresh minced clams, keep the cooking time short, 5 to 10 minutes, or the clams will be tough.

PREP TIME: 5 MINUTES   COOK TIME: 15 MINUTES

Corn & Bean Chowder

MAKES 4 SERVINGS

1/4 cup vegetable oil

2 cups sliced yellow onions

2 teaspoons minced garlic

2 packages (10 ounces each) frozen corn, thawed

4 cups vegetable stock

1/4 teaspoon ground nutmeg

1/2 cup instant milk powder

3/4 cup cooked navy beans

salt and pepper to taste

• Heat the oil in a 6-quart pot, and sauté the onions and garlic until the onions are lightly colored. Add 3 cups of the corn, stock, and nutmeg. Bring to a boil. Reduce to a simmer, cover lightly, and cook, stirring occasionally, until the corn is tender.

• Meanwhile, in the container of a blender or food processor, purée the remaining corn with 1/2 cup of hot liquid from the pot, and process until smooth. Add the milk powder, and stir back into the soup. Add the beans. Bring to a boil, reduce to a simmer, and cook until heated through.

• Turn off the heat, and add salt and pepper to taste. Serve immediately.

PREP TIME: 10 MINUTES   COOK TIME: 1 HOUR, 10 MINUTES

Acorn Squash Chowder

MAKES 6 SERVINGS

3 large carrots, trimmed, peeled, and sliced

1 large red onion, sliced

1/3 cup water

4 acorn squashes, cooked, with pulp and skin
  removed

2 tablespoons butter

1 tablespoon all-purpose flour

2 1/2 cups vegetable stock

1/4 cup unflavored yogurt or sour cream

1/2 cup sherry or white port wine

1/2 teaspoon ground nutmeg

1/8 teaspoon paprika

dash ground allspice

dash of red pepper

1 cup half-and-half

1 1/2 tablespoons brandy (optional)

salt and pepper to taste

- In a 6-quart pot, combine the carrots, onion, and water. Bring to a boil. Reduce to a simmer, cover, and cook for about 15 minutes. Remove from heat and drain.

- In a food process or blender, combine the carrot mixture and squash. Process on high until smooth.

- Melt the butter in a 6-quart pot; sprinkle in the flour, stirring to make a roux. Pouring in a narrow stream, stir in the stock until smooth. Add the yogurt, sherry, nutmeg, paprika, allspice, red pepper, and vegetable purée.

- Bring to a boil, reduce to a simmer, cover, and continue to cook for about 40 minutes. Stir in the half-and-half and brandy, and heat through. Add salt and pepper to taste.

COOKS' TIP:

Most of the alcohol from the port wine and brandy is burned off during cooking, which leaves only the wonderful flavor.

PREP TIME: 5 MINUTES   COOK TIME: 25 MINUTES

Swiss–Butter Bean Chowder

MAKES 4 SERVINGS

Here's a robust chowder that boasts of bacon, Swiss cheese, and plenty of great-tasting vegetables: carrots, cauliflower, butter beans, mustard greens. Fennel seeds add a wonderful anise-like flavor.

2 slices smoked bacon

1 large red onion, chopped

2 cans (14 ounces each) fat-free beef broth

2 cups small cauliflower florets

1 can (15 ounces) butter beans, rinsed and drained

2 carrots, shredded

2 teaspoons white wine vinegar

2 bay leaves

1/2 teaspoon fennel seeds

2 ounces reduced-sodium Swiss cheese, shredded

1/2 cup torn mustard greens

- Sauté the bacon in a 6-quart pot until crisp, about 3 minutes. Transfer to a plate lined with paper towels to drain. Wipe most of the bacon fat from the pot. Add the onion, and sauté until translucent, about 5 minutes.

- Stir in the broth, cauliflower, beans, carrots, vinegar, bay leaves, and fennel seeds. Cover the pot, and bring the mixture to a boil. Reduce the heat, and simmer for 12 minutes. Discard the bay leaves. Stir in the cheese, and heat until it has melted.

- Crumble the bacon. Top each serving with the mustard greens and bacon.

COOKS' TIP:

Don't be tempted to substitute white distilled vinegar for the white wine variety; the distilled variety tastes quite harsh.

[handwritten: 1/19/09.]

[handwritten: 6.5. — a little bland perhaps more chili powder or chili]

[handwritten: takes longer to cook & prep.]

PREP TIME: 10 MINUTES   COOK TIME: 15 MINUTES

Broccoli & Mushroom Chowder

MAKES 6 TO 8 SERVINGS

1 cup butter

1 cup all-purpose flour

4 cups vegetable stock or water

2 pounds fresh broccoli, chopped, steamed until
   tender

8 ounces fresh mushrooms, trimmed and sliced

4 cups half-and-half or milk

1 teaspoon crushed tarragon

salt and pepper to taste

• Melt the butter in a 6-quart pot; sprinkle in the flour, stirring constantly, to make a roux. Add the stock, pouring in a narrow stream, and stirring constantly. Bring to a boil. Reduce to a simmer, add the broccoli, mushrooms, half-and-half, and tarragon. Heat through, but do not allow to boil.

• Turn off the heat, and add salt and pepper to taste. Serve immediately.

PREP TIME: 5 MINUTES   COOK TIME: 20 MINUTES

Chili Chicken Chowder

MAKES 6 SERVINGS

Here's a knockout chowder with signature Southwest flavors: cumin, garlic, and chili. And they play exceptionally well with the basics: chicken, beans, potatoes, carrots, and tomatoes.

1/2 pound cooked chicken breast, cubed

1 can (14 ounces) fat-free chicken broth

1 can (14 ounces) diced tomatoes

1 can (15 ounces) black beans, rinsed and drained

1 red potato, diced

1 large carrot, thinly sliced

2 cloves garlic, minced

1/2 teaspoon cumin seeds

2 teaspoons chili powder

• Combine the chicken, broth, tomatoes, beans, potato, carrot, garlic, cumin seeds, and chili powder in a 6-quart pot. Cover the pot, and bring the mixture to a boil. Reduce the heat, and simmer until the potato and carrot are tender, 15 to 20 minutes.

> **COOKS' TIPS:**
> • Use ground cumin, if you can't get the seeds.
> • Variation: You may substitute turkey for the chicken, and pinto beans for the black beans.

PREP TIME: 5 MINUTES   COOK TIME: 35 MINUTES

Nor'easter Clam Chowder

MAKES 4 SERVINGS

When cold winds blow, warm up with this robust New England style chowder. It holds its own against the elements of hunger, and it's chockablock with flavor from clams, potatoes, corn, and bacon.

3 *slices (about 2 ounces) smoked bacon*

1 *medium onion, chopped*

2 *cans (6¹/2 ounces each) minced clams*

1 *can (11 ounces) clam juice*

2 *medium red potatoes, diced*

³/4 *cup frozen corn*

1¹/2 *cups low-fat (2%) milk*

2 *teaspoons Worcestershire sauce*

³/4 *teaspoon dried savory leaves*

COOKS' TIP:

For a thicker chowder, use less clam juice.

• Cook the bacon in a 3-quart saucepan until browned, about 5 minutes. Transfer to a paper-towel-lined plate to drain. Add the onion to the pan, and sauté until translucent, about 3 minutes.

• Drain the clams, reserving the juice. Add the canned clam juice, the potatoes, and the reserved juice to the pan. Cook the mixture until the potatoes are tender, 15 to 20 minutes.

• Using a slotted spoon, transfer half the mixture to a bowl; cover with foil to keep warm. Using a handheld immersion blender, purée the onion mixture in the pan. Return the reserved vegetables to the pan, and stir in the corn, milk, Worcestershire sauce, savory, and clams.

• Heat the chowder on low (do not boil), stirring occasionally, until it is hot—5 to 10 minutes. Crumble the bacon, and top each serving with it.

PREP TIME: 5 MINUTES   COOK TIME: 15 MINUTES

Corn Chowder

MAKES 8 SERVINGS

2 tablespoons canola oil

1 medium yellow onion, minced

1/2 cup dried potato flakes

3 cups water

1 package (10 ounces) frozen whole-kernel corn,
   thawed

3 cups milk

3 tablespoons butter

salt and pepper to taste

• Heat the oil in a 6-quart pot, and sauté the onion until translucent. Add the potato flakes and water, partly cover, and cook, stirring occasionally, for about 5 minutes.

• Add the corn and milk and continue to simmer for about 5 minutes. Remove from heat. Add the butter and salt and pepper to taste, and serve immediately.

PREP TIME: 10 MINUTES   COOK TIME: 40 MINUTES

Harvest Corn Chowder

MAKES 10 TO 12 SERVINGS

1 tablespoon butter

1 large white onion, chopped

2 cans (14.5 ounces each) cream-style corn

4 cups whole-kernel corn

2 cups diced red potatoes

2 cups diced parsnips

1 can (10.75 ounces) cream-of-mushroom soup

1 can (6 ounces) sliced mushrooms, undrained

3 cups milk

1/2 medium green bell pepper, chopped

1/2 medium red bell pepper, chopped

salt and pepper to taste

● Melt the butter in a 6-quart pot and sauté the onion until tender. Add the cream-style corn, whole corn, potatoes, parsnips, soup, mushrooms, milk, and peppers. Bring to a slow boil, reduce heat immediately to a simmer, partly cover, and cook for about 30 minutes, or until the potatoes and parsnips are fork tender.

● Turn off the heat, and adjust the salt and pepper to taste. Serve immediately.

PREP TIME: 10 MINUTES   COOK TIME: 25 MINUTES

Caribbean Chicken Chowder

MAKES 4 SERVINGS

Fusion cuisine is hot and so is this Caribbean goodie, which boasts Spanish and Cuban influences. Sofrito sauce, hot-pepper sauce, and sunflower seeds give it mouth-watering sizzle.

1 teaspoon olive oil

3/4 pound boneless, skinless chicken breasts,
    cut into 1/2-inch cubes

1 onion, chopped

1 can (14 ounce) fat-free chicken broth

1 can (15 ounces) pigeon peas, rinsed and drained

1 pound tomatoes, chopped

2 cups packed torn chard leaves

2 tablespoons sofrito sauce

1 teaspoon Louisiana hot-pepper sauce

1/4 cup sunflower seeds, toasted

- Warm the oil in a 6-quart pot over medium-high heat for 1 minute. Add the chicken, and sauté until lightly browned, about 5 minutes. Add the onion, and sauté until translucent, about 3 minutes.

- Stir in the broth, peas, and tomatoes. Cover the pot, and bring the mixture to a boil. Reduce the heat, and simmer for 10 minutes. Stir in the chard and sofrito, and cook, uncovered, for 1 minute.

- Stir in the hot-pepper sauce. Top each serving with the sunflower seeds.

COOKS' TIP:

Pigeon peas come in either green or yellow, and can be found in the international section of many supermarkets.

PREP TIME: 10 MINUTES   COOK TIME: 40 MINUTES

Scrod Chowder with Broccoflower

MAKES 4 SERVINGS

A cross between broccoli and cauliflower, broccoflower gives this chowder a splash of bright green color and mild cauliflower flavor.

3 cups cubed peeled potatoes

1 large onion, chopped

1 1/2 cups clam juice

2 bay leaves

2 ounces prosciutto, finely chopped

1/2 teaspoon freshly ground black pepper

2 cups broccoflower florets

1 pound scrod fillet, cut into 1/2-inch pieces

1 cup 2% milk

COOKS' TIP:

Fish is cooked through if the layers are opaque from top to bottom.

• Combine the potatoes, onion, clam juice, and bay leaves in a 6-quart pot. Cover the pot, and bring the mixture to a boil. Reduce the heat, and simmer the mixture until the potatoes are tender, about 15 minutes. Using a slotted spoon, transfer half the potatoes and onions, including the bay leaves, to a bowl; cover with foil to keep the vegetables warm.

• Using a potato masher, mash the vegetables in the pot. Stir in the prosciutto, pepper, and reserved vegetables. Cover the pot, and bring the mixture to a simmer. Add the broccoflower and scrod. Cook, covered, until the broccoflower is tender and the scrod is cooked through, 5 to 10 minutes.

• Stir in the milk and heat the chowder throughout, 3 to 5 minutes. Discard the bay leaves.

PREP TIME: 10 MINUTES   COOK TIME: 35 MINUTES

Cheesy Chowder

MAKES 2 SERVINGS

1/4 cup butter, at room temperature

1/3 cup all-purpose flour

4 cups vegetable stock

1 1/2 cups diced potatoes

1 cup diced celery

1 cup diced carrots

1/2 cup diced yellow onions

3 cups milk

1 tablespoon soy sauce

8 ounces processed cheese spread, cubed

salt and pepper

COOKS' TIP:

This is a chowder lover's dream come true. Its flavor can easily be changed with the type of cheese used.

● In a cup or small bowl, using the back of a spoon, blend the butter and flour together; set aside.

● In a 6-quart pot, combine the stock, potatoes, celery, carrots, and onions. Bring to a boil, reduce to a simmer, and cover. Cook, stirring occasionally, for about 20 minutes, or until the potatoes are tender.

● In a saucepan, melt the flour mixture to make a roux. Add the milk, pouring in a narrow stream and stirring constantly. Cook, stirring constantly, until thickened.

● Stir the milk mixture into the cooking vegetables; add the soy sauce and cheese. Continue to cook, stirring frequently, until the cheese has melted.

● Turn off the heat, and add salt and pepper to taste. Serve immediately.

Bean & Legume Soups

PREP TIME: 10 MINUTES, PLUS 1 HOUR TO SIT   COOK TIME: 1 HOUR 20 MINUTES

Bean Lover's Soup

MAKES 8 SERVINGS

Cause a stir with this super mixed-bean soup. It's flavored with carrots, spinach, and ham, and makes for a substantial meal in a bowl.

16 ounces bean soup mix (mixed dried beans)

2 cans (14 ounces each) fat-free beef broth

2 cups water

2 carrots, sliced

2 cups torn fresh spinach

2 ounces deli baked ham, cut into 1/4-inch cubes

1 teaspoon tarragon leaves

1/2 teaspoon lemon pepper

paprika, for garnish

parsley sprigs, for garnish

COOKS' TIP:

If you'd prefer not to wait an hour for the beans to soak in hot water, soak them in cold water in the refrigerator overnight instead.

• Rinse the beans and sort through them to remove debris. Place the beans in an 8-quart pot and add 6 cups water. Cover the pot and bring the water to a boil. Simmer for 3 minutes. Remove the pot from the heat. Let sit for 1 hour. Drain the beans and return them to the pot.

• Add the broth, 2 cups water, carrots, spinach, ham, tarragon, and lemon pepper. Cover the pot, and bring the mixture to a boil. Reduce the heat, and simmer until the beans are tender, about 11/4 hours.

• Transfer half the mixture to a bowl; cover the bowl to keep the mixture hot. Using a handheld immersion blender, purée the mixture in the pot. Return the reserved mixture to the pot. Heat the soup throughout, about 5 minutes; do not boil. Top each serving with the paprika and parsley.

Navy Bean Soup with Shallots

MAKES 4 SERVINGS

This super-satisfying soup is creamy and rich tasting—thanks to puréed navy beans, Madeira wine, and Romano cheese.

8 ounces dried navy beans

2 teaspoons olive oil

3 medium (about 6 ounces) shallots, chopped

1 carrot, diced

1 celery stalk, sliced

1/4 cup Madeira wine

2³/4 cups reduced-sodium vegetable broth

1 teaspoon dried rosemary

1/4 cup grated Romano cheese

1/4 cup snipped fresh parsley

COOKS' TIP:

Too rushed to cook beans? Then use 3 cups of rinsed and drained canned white beans instead.

● Rinse and sort the beans. Place the beans and 3 cups water in a 6-quart pot. Cover the pot, and bring to a boil. Reduce the heat, and simmer for 3 minutes. Remove from the heat and let sit for 1 hour. Drain the beans and return them to the pot. Add 4 cups of water. Cover the pot, and bring to a boil. Reduce the heat, and simmer until the beans are tender, about 1 hour. Drain.

● Warm the oil in the same 6-quart pot over medium-high heat for 1 minute. Add the shallots, carrot, and celery, and cook until the vegetables are soft, about 6 minutes. Stir in the Madeira and ³/4 cup broth, and cook 6 minutes over medium heat.

● Stir in the beans, remaining 2 cups of broth, and rosemary. Cover the pot, and bring the mixture to a boil. Reduce the heat, and simmer for 5 minutes. Using a slotted spoon, transfer half the mixture to a bowl; cover to keep the vegetables warm. Using a handheld immersion blender, purée the mixture in the pot. Stir in the reserved vegetables, Romano, and parsley. Heat until the soup is hot throughout, about 2 minutes.

PREP TIME: 5 MINUTES   COOK TIME: 30 MINUTES

Black-Eyed Pea & Corn Soup

MAKES 4 SERVINGS

Here's a hearty, homey soup that's high in flavor and low in fat. Smoked bacon, roasted red peppers, garlic, thyme, and fresh parsley punch up flavor and color.

4 slices smoked bacon
2 cups fat-free chicken broth
1 can (15 ounces) black-eyed peas, rinsed
   and drained
1 can (14 ounces) cream-style corn
1 cup chopped red onions
4 cloves garlic
1 teaspoon dried thyme
1/4 teaspoon white pepper
1 cup roasted red peppers
1/4 cup snipped fresh parsley

- Cook the bacon in a 3-quart saucepan over medium-high heat until browned. Transfer to a paper-towel-lined plate to drain.

- Add the broth, black-eyed peas, corn, onions, garlic, thyme, and white pepper to the saucepan. Cover the pot, and bring the mixture to a boil. Reduce the heat, and simmer for 15 minutes to blend the flavors.

- Stir in the roasted peppers, and heat the soup for 1 minute more. Crumble the bacon. Top each serving of soup with bacon and parsley.

COOKS' TIP:

If you are out of red onion, use a sweet onion.

PREP TIME: 10 MINUTES   COOK TIME: 30 MINUTES

Curried Bean Soup

MAKES 4 SERVINGS

Here I offer an elegant, creamy soup with a soft yellow color and subtle curry flavor. It's easy to make as well.

2 cans (14 ounces each) fat-free chicken broth

1 cup canned garbanzo beans, rinsed and drained

1 cup canned great northern beans, rinsed
   and drained

1 medium potato, peeled and diced

1 leek, white part only, sliced

1 celery stalk, sliced

2 cloves garlic, chopped

2 teaspoons white wine vinegar

1/2 teaspoon curry powder

1 cup 2% milk

1/2 cup shredded reduced-sodium cheddar cheese

1/2 cup snipped fresh parsley

• Combine the broth, garbanzo beans, great northern beans, potato, leek, celery, garlic, vinegar, and curry powder in a 6-quart pot. Cover the pot, and bring the mixture to a boil. Reduce the heat, and simmer for 15 minutes.

• Remove from the heat. Using a handheld immersion blender, purée the mixture. Stir in the milk and cheddar. Return the soup to the heat, and warm it until the cheddar has melted and the soup is hot throughout (do not boil), 3 to 5 minutes. Top each serving with parsley.

COOKS' TIPS:

• If you don't have an immersion blender, let the soup cool just enough to pour it safely into a regular blender. Process the soup and return it to the pot.
• For a slightly more pronounced color, use yellow cheddar cheese.

PREP TIME: 5 MINUTES   COOK TIME: 35 MINUTES

Baked Bean Soup

MAKES 4 SERVINGS

It was once said that the way beans are prepared nearly defined the Mason-Dixon Line. In the North they were prepared in one way, and in the South another way. This soup marries both cuisines.

3 tablespoons butter

1/2 cup chopped yellow onion

1 medium clove garlic, minced

3 tablespoons all-purpose flour

1/4 teaspoon dry mustard

2 cups tomato juice or V-8 vegetable juice

1 cup vegetable stock or water

2 teaspoons Worcestershire sauce

1 can (21 ounces) baked beans

salt and pepper to taste

shredded cheddar cheese for garnish

● Melt the butter in a 6-quart pot, and sauté the onion and garlic together until the onion is translucent. Sprinkle in the flour and mustard powder, stirring to make a roux. Pouring in a narrow stream, stir in the tomato juice and stock until smooth. Add the Worcestershire sauce and beans, partly cover, and cook, stirring frequently, until thickened. Reduce to a simmer and continue to cook, undisturbed, for about 30 minutes.

● Turn off the heat, and add salt and pepper to taste. Serve immediately garnished with cheese.

PREP TIME: 10 MINUTES   COOK TIME: 30 MINUTES

Fresh Swiss Chard & Snap Bean Soup

MAKES 4 SERVINGS

Heads up, garlic lovers: This soup is brazen, bold, and assertive with the wonderful flavors of garlic and Swiss chard.

4 slices bacon

2 cans (14 ounces each) fat-free beef broth

4 large (or 8 medium) cloves garlic, thinly sliced

1/2 pound fresh green beans, cut into 1-inch lengths

1 small zucchini, quartered and sliced

4 ounces Swiss chard leaves, torn, stems removed

1/4 teaspoon white pepper

1 sprig thyme

● Cook the bacon in a nonstick skillet over medium-high heat until crisp. Transfer the bacon to a paper-towel-lined plate to drain. Let the bacon cool; crumble it.

● Pour the broth into a 6-quart pot. Stir in the garlic, beans, zucchini, chard, pepper, and thyme. Cover the pot, and bring the mixture to a boil. Reduce the heat, and simmer until the vegetables are tender, about 20 minutes. Discard the thyme. Serve garnished with the bacon.

COOKS' TIP:

The fastest way to cut fresh green beans into 1-inch pieces is to "snap" them. Or you can line up several, about half a dozen is good, on a cutting board and cut all six beans at once.

PREP TIME: 10 MINUTES COOK TIME: 25 MINUTES

Chili Bean Soup with Summer Squash

MAKES 4 SERVINGS

Few dishes are faster, easier, or tastier than this chunky bean soup, which features fresh tomatoes, squash, and cilantro. It's ready to eat in just 20 minutes.

2 cans (14 ounces each) fat-free beef broth

1 large onion, chopped

2 carrots, thinly sliced

1 medium yellow summer squash, halved and sliced

3 cups canned chili beans with liquid

2 cups fresh tomatoes, chopped

1/4 teaspoon freshly ground black pepper

1 teaspoon dried cilantro

● Combine the broth, onion, carrots, and squash in a 6-quart pot. Cover the pot, and bring the mixture to a boil. Reduce the heat, and simmer until the carrots are almost tender, about 10 minutes.

● Stir in the chili beans, tomatoes, and pepper, and simmer the mixture for 5 minutes more. Stir in the cilantro.

COOKS' TIP:

Variation: You may substitute fat-free chicken broth for the beef broth and zucchini for the yellow summer squash.

PREP TIME: 10 MINUTES COOK TIME: 30 MINUTES

Garbanzo Bean Soup with Pepperoni

MAKES 6 SERVINGS

Pepperoni makes this uncommonly delicious soup really sing and perks up the basics: potatoes, sweet peppers, and garbanzo beans (or chickpeas, as they're known in many cooking circles).

4 cups fat-free beef broth

1 large potato, chopped

2 celery stalks, sliced

4 teaspoons dried minced onion

1 teaspoon cumin seeds

1/2 teaspoon dried thyme

1 can (15 ounces) garbanzo beans, rinsed and drained

1 small sweet yellow pepper, chopped

2 tablespoons diced cooked pepperoni

● Combine the broth, potato, celery, onion, cumin, and thyme in a 6-quart pot. Cover the pot, and bring the mixture to a boil. Reduce the heat, and simmer for 12 minutes. Stir in the beans, pepper, and pepperoni. Simmer for 8 minutes.

COOKS' TIP:

By cooking and dicing pepperoni, you can maximize its flavor while minimizing its fat.

6-24-08 Had w/o pepperoni. Green Tabasco + Chipotle Tabasco good. Bleu cheese crumbles made it VERY GOOD!

PREP TIME: 5 MINUTES   COOK TIME: 30 MINUTES

Zucchini-Cannellini Soup

MAKES 4 SERVINGS

It's amazing how much intriguing flavor just a smidgen of smoked Lebanon bologna can add to this soul-satisfying soup.

2 teaspoons olive oil

1 can (16 ounces) low-sodium cannellini beans, rinsed and drained

1 small zucchini, thinly sliced

4 scallions, sliced

2 cloves garlic, minced

1 cup water

1 cup fat-free beef broth

1 slice (1 ounce) smoked Lebanon bologna, chopped

1/4 teaspoon white pepper

1/4 teaspoon celery seeds

snipped fresh parsley, for garnish

● Warm the oil in a 3-quart saucepan over medium-high heat. Add the beans, zucchini, scallions, and garlic, and cook until the zucchini is translucent, 8 to 10 minutes.

● Transfer half the vegetable mixture to a food processor and purée it. Return the mixture to the saucepan. Pour in the water and beef broth. Stir in the bologna, pepper, and celery seeds. Cover the pot and bring the mixture to a boil. Reduce the heat, and simmer the soup for 15 minutes. Garnish each serving with parsley.

Indian Tomato Lentil Soup

PREP TIME: 5 MINUTES   COOK TIME: 35 MINUTES

MAKES 4 SERVINGS

2 tablespoons virgin olive oil

1 medium red onion, chopped

1 teaspoon ground coriander

3/4 teaspoon ground turmeric

3/4 teaspoon ground cumin

light pinch curry powder

pinch ground cloves

4 cups vegetable stock

1 can (16 ounces) chopped tomatoes

1 package (12 ounces) dried red lentils, rinsed
  and drained

• Heat the oil in a saucepan, and sauté the onion until translucent. Add the coriander, turmeric, cumin, curry powder, cloves, stock, tomatoes, and lentils. Bring to a boil. Reduce to a simmer, cover lightly, and cook, stirring, for 20 to 30 minutes, or until the lentils are very tender.

• Remove from heat, and purée in batches, using a blender or food processor. Return to the saucepan, heat through, and serve.

Garbanzo Bean & Spinach Soup

PREP TIME: 10 MINUTES   COOK TIME: 30 MINUTES

MAKES ABOUT 4 SERVINGS

1 tablespoon butter

1 large yellow onion, chopped

4 small cloves garlic, minced

1 cup milk

1 can (16 ounces) garbanzo beans,
  drained and rinsed

4 to 5 cups fresh spinach, shredded

1/8 teaspoon cardamom powder

1/8 teaspoon ground nutmeg

1 teaspoon curry powder

1/4 teaspoon ground turmeric

salt and pepper to taste

• Melt the butter in a 4-quart pot, and sauté the onion and garlic until the onion is translucent. Stir in the milk, and bring to a boil. Then reduce to a simmer, add the garbanzo beans, spinach, cardamom, nutmeg, curry powder, and turmeric, and cook, stirring occasionally, for about 15 minutes.

• Transfer about 1 1/2 cups of the soup to the container of a blender, and purée until smooth. Return to the pot, and heat through.

• Turn off the heat, and add salt and pepper to taste. Serve immediately.

PREP TIME: 10 MINUTES   COOK TIME: 25 MINUTES

Easy Cannellini Bean & Potato Soup

MAKES 6 SERVINGS

Hankering for a comforting, hearty soup that is ready in a flash? Satisfy your cravings with this simply seasoned soup of beans, carrots, and potatoes. Tasters enjoyed it, and I think it'll more than meet your expectations.

2 cans (14 ounces each) fat-free beef broth

1 can (15 ounces) cannellini beans, rinsed and drained

1 large potato, peeled and diced

1 large onion, chopped

1 celery stalk, sliced

1 carrot, diced

2 bay leaves

1 teaspoon red wine vinegar

1/2 teaspoon fennel seeds

1/4 teaspoon freshly ground black pepper

1 cup croutons, for garnish

1/4 cup snipped fresh cilantro, for garnish

● Combine the broth, beans, potato, onion, celery, carrot, bay leaves, vinegar, fennel, and black pepper in a 6-quart pot. Cover the pot, and bring the mixture to a boil. Reduce the heat, and simmer until the potatoes are tender, about 15 minutes. Discard the bay leaves.

● Transfer about half the vegetables to a bowl. Using a handheld immersion blender, purée the vegetables in the pot. Return the reserved vegetables to the pot. Serve the soup garnished with croutons and cilantro.

COOKS' TIP:

For directions on making croutons, see the Cooks' Tip under French Onion Soup, page 130.

PREP TIME: 5 MINUTES   COOK TIME: 20 MINUTES

Great Northern–Cauliflower Soup

MAKES 4 SERVINGS

Puréed beans and potatoes are the secret behind the low-fat "creamy" texture of this superb soup. For contrasting texture, serve the soup with crunchy croutons, crusty bread, or crisp crackers.

1 can (14 ounces) fat-free chicken broth

1 can (14 ounces) great northern beans, rinsed and drained

1 potato, peeled and cut into 1/2-inch cubes

1/2 pound cauliflower, cut into small florets

1 teaspoon minced dried onion

1/4 teaspoon celery seed

1/4 teaspoon freshly ground black pepper

1 cup skim milk

1/2 cup shredded Monterey Jack cheese

paprika, for garnish

● Pour the broth into a 6-quart pot; add the beans, potato, cauliflower, onion, celery seed, and black pepper. Cover the pot and bring the mixture to a boil. Reduce the heat and simmer the mixture until the vegetables are tender, about 12 minutes.

● Using a slotted spoon, transfer half the vegetables to a bowl; keep them warm. With a handheld immersion blender, purée the vegetables in the pot. Stir in the reserved vegetables, milk, and Monterey Jack cheese.

● Cover the pot and heat the soup over a low flame until it is hot throughout, about 5 minutes. Serve garnished with the paprika.

PREP TIME: 10 MINUTES   COOK TIME: 30 MINUTES

Two Bean & Corn Chili Soup

MAKES 8 SERVINGS

This extra-easy, all-vegetable soup has the intense flavors of a hearty chili. For some crunch, serve it with baked tortilla chips.

1 large onion, chopped

1 medium green sweet pepper, chopped

3 cloves garlic, minced

1 1/2 cups corn

1 poblano pepper, minced

1 can (28 ounces) crushed tomatoes

1 can (14 ounces) fat-free beef broth

1 can (15 ounces) red kidney beans, rinsed and drained

1 can (16 ounces) black beans, rinsed and drained

2 tablespoons chili powder

1 teaspoon ground cumin

1/4 teaspoon ground allspice

● Cook the onion, sweet pepper, and garlic in a 4-quart nonstick pot over medium heat until the onion is translucent, about 7 minutes.

● Stir in the corn, poblano, tomatoes, broth, beans, chili powder, cumin, and allspice. Cover the pot, and bring the mixture to a boil. Reduce the heat, and simmer the soup for 20 minutes.

COOKS' TIP:

Don't have a nonstick pot? Then coat the bottom of a regular pot with nonstick cooking spray before cooking the onion, pepper, and garlic.

PREP TIME: 10 MINUTES   COOK TIME: 35 MINUTES

Hearty Minestrone with Elbow Macaroni

MAKES 4 SERVINGS

Minestrone means "big soup" in Italian, and traditional versions overflow with pasta, beans, and other robust vegetables. This easy version lives up to its namesake.

1 carrot, thinly sliced

1 celery stalk, sliced

1 cup cut green beans

2/3 cup sliced scallions

1 can (14 ounces) low-sodium vegetable broth

1 teaspoon Italian herb seasoning

1 can (16 ounces) stewed tomatoes

pinch of cayenne pepper

1 tablespoon red wine vinegar

1/2 cup elbow macaroni

1/2 cup snipped fresh parsley

Parmesan cheese (optional)

• Combine the carrot, celery, beans, scallions, broth, Italian herb seasoning, tomatoes, pepper, and vinegar in a 6-quart pot. Cover the pot, and bring to a boil. Reduce the heat, and simmer for 25 minutes.

• Stir in the macaroni, and cook the mixture for 7 minutes more. Serve the soup topped with parsley and Parmesan, if desired.

COOKS' TIP:

Planning to double this recipe and serve half another time? Then divide the soup before adding the macaroni only to the portion you are serving right away. Pasta tends to oversoften when stored in a broth.

1-2-08: Doubled recipe. Soup delicious; flavorful. May try with white beans next time.

The best!

Split Pea Soup

MAKES 4 SERVINGS

Here's an updated and easy version of old-fashioned comfort food, and it's full to the brim with split peas, smoked ham, leeks, and carrots. What else has it got? Less than 2 grams of fat and lots of fiber.

8 ounces green split peas

2 cans (14 ounces each) fat-free beef broth

1 cup water

2 ounces cooked smoked ham, chopped

1 cup chopped leeks, white parts only

1 cup diced carrots

2 bay leaves

1/4 teaspoon lemon pepper

1/2 teaspoon ground coriander

2 tablespoons snipped fresh parsley

COOKS' TIP:

If you're rushed, you can skip soaking the split peas, but be aware that you may need to cook them a few minutes longer.

• Pour 3 cups water into a 6-quart pot. Add the split peas. Cover the pot, and bring the mixture to a boil. Reduce the heat, and simmer for 3 minutes. Remove the pot from the heat and let the peas soak for 1 hour. Drain the peas and return them to the pot.

• Stir in the broth, 1 cup water, ham, leeks, carrots, bay leaves, lemon pepper, and coriander. Cover the pot, and bring the mixture to a boil. Reduce the heat, and simmer until the peas are tender, 45 to 60 minutes. Discard the bay leaves. Transfer half the vegetables to a bowl; cover it with foil to keep the vegetables warm.

• Using a handheld immersion blender, purée the mixture in the pot. Return the reserved vegetables to the pot. Heat until the soup is hot throughout, about 3 minutes. Top each serving with parsley.

PREP TIME: 10 MINUTES, PLUS OVERNIGHT SOAK   COOK TIME: 3 HOURS

Bean Soup with Pistou

MAKES 4 TO 6 SERVINGS

1 cup dried navy beans

1 cup dried cannellini beans

1 large yellow onion, chopped

5 cups boiling vegetable stock

2 large carrots, peeled and minced

1 cup shredded cabbage

2 small red potatoes, peeled and diced

1 package (10 ounces) frozen cut green beans,
   thawed

salt and pepper

PISTOU

1/4 cup minced garlic

3 tablespoons chopped basil leaves

6 tablespoons virgin olive oil

1/4 cup grated fresh Romano cheese

● The night before, place the navy beans and cannellini beans in separate large bowls or saucepans. Cover with cold water, and set aside until needed.

● When ready, position the rack in the center of the oven and preheat to 400°F. Drain the soaked beans, and rinse several times. Place together in a large bean pot or saucepan. Add the onion and enough water to cover the beans. Cover tightly, and cook in the oven for 1 1/2 to 2 hours, or until the beans are very tender.

● Remove from the oven and drain. Using a blender or food processor, purée the mixture in batches until smooth. Return to the bean pot, slowly add the vegetable stock, carrots, cabbage, chopped potatoes, and green beans. Add salt and pepper to taste, cover again, and return the pot to the oven. Reduce the heat to 350°F and cook for an additional 1 hour.

● Meanwhile, using a mortar and pestle, or a small bowl and large spoon, pound the garlic and basil together until very smooth. Gradually blend in the oil, and stir in the cheese.

● Remove the soup from the oven, and stir in one half of the pistou. Ladle into warmed bowls, and serve with the remaining pistou on the side.

Lentil Soup with Prosciutto

MAKES 4 SERVINGS

Prosciutto and Provolone cheese provide the pizzazz that sets this singular soup apart.

1 cup lentils

2 cans (14 ounces each) fat-free beef broth

1 medium red potato, diced

1 medium onion, chopped

2 stalks celery, sliced

2 cloves garlic, crushed

2 ounces thinly sliced prosciutto, chopped

1/4 teaspoon freshly ground black pepper

1 cup packed torn fresh spinach

1/3 cup shredded reduced-sodium Provolone cheese

2 tablespoons fresh oregano leaves

- Fill a 6-quart pot with water. Add the lentils. Cover the pot, and bring the mixture to a boil. Reduce the heat, and simmer for 3 minutes. Remove from the heat and let sit for 30 to 60 minutes.

- Drain the lentils, and return them to the pot. Stir in the broth, potato, onion, celery, garlic, prosciutto, and pepper. Cover the pot, and bring the mixture to a boil. Reduce the heat, and simmer until the lentils and potatoes are tender, 12 to 15 minutes.

- Stir in the spinach and Provolone cheese. Top each serving with oregano.

COOKS' TIP:

Lentils don't have to be soaked before they're cooked. If you skip that step, simply increase the cooking time by 30 to 45 minutes.

Quick Fava Bean Soup

MAKES 4 SERVINGS

Buttery-tasting fava beans and fresh tomatoes steal the show in this robust shortcut soup.

1 teaspoon olive oil

1 medium onion, chopped

4 cloves garlic

1 can (14 ounces) fava beans, rinsed and drained

1 medium yellow summer squash, chopped

2 3/4 cups fat-free beef broth

2 cups diced plum tomatoes

4 ounces Canadian bacon, chopped

1 teaspoon Italian herb seasoning

1 teaspoon red wine vinegar

• Warm the oil in a 6-quart pot for 1 minute over medium-high heat. Add onion and garlic, and sauté them until the onion is golden. Add the beans, squash, broth, tomatoes, bacon, herb seasoning, and vinegar. Cover the pot, and bring the mixture to a boil. Reduce the heat and simmer until the squash is tender, about 15 minutes.

Shell Soup with Roman Beans

MAKES 4 SERVINGS

When your taste buds call out for an earthy, country-style soup, try this pasta-and-bean version. It's fast. It's easy. And it's richly flavored—with ham, anchovies, and Provolone cheese.

2 cans (14 ounces each) fat-free beef broth

2 carrots, thinly sliced

1 small onion, chopped

1 can (15 ounces) Roman beans, rinsed and drained

4 ounces pasta shells

1/4 pound reduced-sodium deli ham, diced

1/2 can (1 ounce) anchovies, drained and mashed

1/4 teaspoon crushed red pepper flakes

1/2 cup grated reduced-sodium Provolone cheese

• Combine broth, carrots, and onion in a 6-quart pot. Cover the pot, and bring the mixture to a boil. Reduce the heat, and simmer for 5 minutes. Add beans, shells, ham, anchovies, and pepper. Simmer the mixture for 14 minutes. Stir in the Provolone, and cook for 1 minute more.

COOKS' TIP:

Having trouble finding Roman beans? Then look for cranberry beans; sometimes that's the way they're labeled.

PREP TIME: 10 MINUTES   COOK TIME: 30 MINUTES

Cabbage Bean Soup with Rivels

MAKES 6 SERVINGS

Rivels are small chunks of homemade pasta or very tiny dumplings. Flavor the rivels by sprinkling them with finely chopped or ground basil or another herb.

RIVELS

1 cup all-purpose flour

2 tablespoons milk

1 egg, beaten

4 cups water or vegetable stock

5 cups shredded green cabbage

1¹/₃ cups shredded carrots

2 tablespoons bacon bits

1 tablespoon Herb Ox vegetable bouillon granules

1 tablespoon cider vinegar

1 teaspoon caraway seeds

1 large onion, chopped

1 medium apple, coarsely chopped

1 can (15.5 ounces) great northern beans, rinsed

salt and pepper to taste

● To make the rivels, in a bowl, using a fork or pastry blender, combine the flour, milk, and egg until coarse crumbs (about the size of raisins) form. Set aside.

● In a 6-quart pot, combine the water, cabbage, carrots, bacon bits, bouillon granules, vinegar, caraway seeds, onion, apple, and beans. Bring to a boil, then reduce to a simmer, partly cover, and cook for about 5 minutes.

● Sprinkle in the rivels, stirring to separate them, and cover the pot again. Continue to simmer for about 20 minutes or until the vegetables are tender.

● Turn off the heat, and add salt and pepper to taste. Serve immediately.

PREP TIME: 10 MINUTES, PLUS OVERNIGHT SOAK   COOK TIME: 3 HOURS 30 MINUTES

Black Bean Soup

MAKES 6 SERVINGS

1 pound dried black beans, soaked in water overnight

2 whole bay leaves

3 quarts vegetable stock or water

1 cup olive or canola oil

3 small shallots, diced

1 small white onion, diced

1 large red pepper, trimmed, seeded, and diced

1 large green pepper, trimmed, seeded, and diced

3 cloves garlic, minced

1 tablespoon ground cumin

2 teaspoons crushed dried oregano

2 tablespoons chopped fresh parsley

2 tablespoons light brown sugar

salt and pepper to taste

• Drain the soaking beans. Transfer them to a 6-quart pot. Add the bay leaves and stock, and bring to a boil. Then reduce to a simmer, partially cover, and cook, stirring occasionally, for 2½ to 3 hours, or until the beans are very tender. Add more water if necessary during cooking.

• Meanwhile, heat the oil in a skillet and sauté the shallots and onion until translucent. Add the red pepper, green pepper, and garlic, and continue to cook, stirring frequently, for about 3 minutes. Add the cumin, oregano, and parsley. Heat through and add the sugar. Remove from heat and cool slightly.

• In the container of a blender or food processor, purée the sautéed ingredients until smooth. Stir into the cooking beans. Cover again, and continue to cook for an additional 30 minutes.

• Turn off the heat, remove and discard the bay leaves, and add salt and pepper to taste. Serve immediately.

PREP TIME: 5 MINUTES   COOK TIME: 35 MINUTES

Drunken Bean Soup

MAKES 6 SERVINGS

2 cans (15 ounces each) pinto beans,
   drained and rinsed

1/2 cup beer

1 1/2 cups vegetable stock

1/2 medium yellow onion, sliced

3 medium cloves garlic, minced

1/2 cup fresh cilantro leaves

1 fresh jalapeño pepper, sliced thin

salt and pepper to taste

● In a 6-quart pot, combine the beans, beer, stock, onion, garlic, cilantro, and pepper. Bring to a boil. Reduce to a simmer, cover lightly, and cook for about 30 minutes, or until the beans are tender.

● Turn off the heat, and add salt and pepper to taste. Serve immediately.

PREP TIME: 10 MINUTES   COOK TIME: 25 MINUTES

Black-Eyed Peas & Watercress Soup

MAKES 6 SERVINGS

1 teaspoon extra virgin olive oil

1 large yellow onion, chopped

2 large carrots, peeled and chopped

4 medium garlic cloves, chopped

4 cans (15 ounces each) black-eyed peas, drained

8 cups vegetable stock

1/2 pound fresh watercress

salt and pepper to taste

● Heat the oil in a 6-quart pot, and sauté the onion until translucent. Add the carrots and garlic, heat through, and then add the beans and stock. Bring to a boil and reduce to a simmer. Cook, stirring occasionally, for 7 to 8 minutes, or until the vegetables are tender.

● Meanwhile, thoroughly wash the watercress, and discard any discolored leaves and stems. Separate about 2 cups (loosely packed) of the tender watercress sprigs, and coarsely chop the remaining watercress.

● Remove the soup from heat. Transfer 1 cup of the solid ingredients to a bowl. In the container of a blender, purée the remaining soup in batches, until smooth.

● Return the purée and the reserved solids to the pan, and bring to a boil. Remove from heat, stir in the watercress sprigs and pieces, and add salt and pepper to taste. Ladle into heated bowls. Serve immediately.

Tex-Mex Black Bean Soup with Jalapeños

MAKES 6 SERVINGS

This soup is south-of-the-border hot and spicy. Dried chili powder will be hotter than fresh red chiles.

2 tablespoons vegetable oil

2 medium yellow onions, chopped

4 medium cloves garlic, minced

8 jalapeños, seeded and chopped

1 tablespoon fresh red chili, crushed; or dried
　red chili powder

2 cups dried black beans, soaked in water overnight
　and drained

1 cup canned diced tomatoes

2 teaspoons ground cumin

1 teaspoon ground epazote*

1 teaspoon ground coriander

1/4 teaspoon ground cloves

1 tablespoon red wine vinegar

6 to 8 cups water

3 tablespoons tequila (optional)

sour cream, for garnish

• Heat the oil in a saucepan, and sauté the onions and garlic together until the onions are tender.

• In a 6-quart pot, combine the onions and garlic with the jalapeños, red chili, beans, tomatoes, cumin, epazote, coriander, cloves, vinegar, and water. Bring to a boil. Reduce to a simmer, partly cover, and cook for about 2 hours, or until the beans are tender.

• In the container of a blender or food processor, purée one half of the soup until smooth. Pour the puréed portion back into the hot mixture, and continue to simmer for about 15 minutes, or until thickened to desired consistency.

• Turn off the heat, and stir in the tequila. Serve immediately with a garnish of sour cream on the side.

COOKS' TIP:

Since jalapeños and other chili peppers can burn the skin, wear gloves while handling them.
*Epazote is also sold under the name Mexican tea and wormseed.

PREP TIME: 10 MINUTES, PLUS OVERNIGHT SOAK   COOK TIME: 3 HOURS

Black Bean Soup
with Turnips

MAKES 6 SERVINGS

1 pound dried black beans, soaked in water overnight
  and drained

8 cups water

2 teaspoons celery salt

2 cups vegetable stock

2 pounds turnips, peeled and finely diced

1 1/4 tablespoons olive oil

1 1/2 cups green peppers, seeded and chopped

1 1/2 cups minced red onions

1 1/4 tablespoons crushed garlic

1 teaspoon ground cumin

1 can (16 ounces) diced tomatoes with juice

1/4 cup red wine vinegar

salt and pepper to taste

COOKS' TIP:

The secret of this combination is to dice the turnips very small. That way, they add to the soup's texture.

• In a 6-quart pot, combine the beans, water, and celery salt. Bring to a boil, reduce to a simmer, and partly cover. Cook, stirring occasionally, for about 2 1/4 hours, or until the beans are very tender.

• Drain the beans through a fine sieve, reserving the liquid. Add the stock to the reserved liquid, putting the beans and stock back into the pot. Add the turnips and bring to a boil. Reduce to a simmer, and continue to cook, stirring occasionally, for about 10 minutes.

• Heat the oil in a skillet and sauté the peppers, onions, garlic, and cumin, stirring constantly, until the onions are a golden color. Add the tomatoes and vinegar. Reduce the heat to the lowest setting, cover, and cook for about 15 minutes. Stir the tomato mixture into the beans, and heat through.

• Turn off the heat, and add salt and pepper to taste. Serve immediately.

PREP TIME: 10 MINUTES, PLUS OVERNIGHT SOAK   COOK TIME: 2 HOURS 30 MINUTES

Black Bean Soup with Orange

MAKES ABOUT 6 SERVINGS

2 cups dried black beans, soaked in water overnight

7 cups water

2 Herb Ox Vegetable bouillon cubes

freshly ground pepper

2 leeks, sliced

2 medium carrots, peeled and chopped

1 medium yellow onion, chopped

1/4 cup fresh chopped cilantro

1 cup fresh orange juice

2 tablespoons orange zest

COOKS' TIP:

For best results, use Herb Ox cubes rather than the granules.

• Drain the beans, and put them in a 6-quart pot. Add 5 cups of water, bouillon cubes, and pepper. Bring to a boil. Reduce to a simmer, cover lightly, and cook, stirring occasionally, for 2 to 2$1/2$ hours, or until the beans are very tender.

• Meanwhile, in a saucepan, combine the leeks, carrots, and onion. Add the remaining 2 cups of water, and bring to a boil. Reduce to a simmer, and cook until the carrots are tender.

• Remove 2 cups of cooked beans and liquid from the pot, and purée in the container of a blender or food processor. Stir back into the pot of beans.

• Add the cooked vegetables with their cooking water to the beans, and bring to a boil. Remove from heat, stir in the cilantro, orange juice, and orange zest. Serve immediately.

British Two-Bean Soup

MAKES 6 SERVINGS

1 tablespoon butter

1 small white onion, chopped

1 medium clove garlic, minced

4 cups vegetable stock

2 teaspoons tomato sauce

1 package (5 ounces) dried lima beans, soaked
   overnight

1 package (2.5 ounces) dried white beans, soaked
   overnight

1 can (8 ounces) diced tomatoes

1 tablespoon packed light brown sugar

1 teaspoon crushed sage

1/2 cup enriched soy milk

1 tablespoon evaporated milk

salt and pepper to taste

• Melt the butter in a saucepan or large pot, and sauté the onion and garlic together until the onion is translucent. Add the stock, tomato sauce, lima beans, and diced tomatoes. Bring to a boil, reduce to a simmer, cover lightly, and cook, stirring occasionally, about 1 hour 30 minutes, until the beans are tender.

• Remove from heat and purée in batches, using a blender or food processor, until smooth. Return to the pot, and add the white beans, sugar, and sage. Simmer over low heat for about 40 minutes, or until the white beans are tender. Add more water if necessary during cooking.

• Remove from heat. Stir in the soy milk and evaporated milk, and add salt and pepper to taste. Serve immediately.

PREP TIME: 5 MINUTES   COOK TIME: 30 MINUTES

Smoky Garbanzo & Tomato Soup

MAKES 6 SERVINGS

Lebanon bologna and Marsala wine pair up to give this extra-easy soup an intriguing smoky flavor. Better prepare an extra batch; dining companions are likely to want seconds.

2 cans (14 ounces each) fat-free chicken broth

2 potatoes, peeled and diced

1 can (14 ounces) garbanzo beans, rinsed
    and drained

1 can (14 ounces) fire-roasted diced tomatoes*

4 cloves garlic, chopped

2 scallions, thinly sliced

2 ounces Lebanon bologna, chopped

1/4 teaspoon freshly ground black pepper

1/4 teaspoon ground celery seed

1 tablespoon Marsala wine

snipped parsley, for garnish

● In a large pot, combine the broth, potatoes, beans, tomatoes, garlic, scallions, bologna, pepper, celery seed, and wine. Cover, and bring the mixture to a boil. Reduce the heat, and simmer until the potatoes are tender, about 20 minutes.

● Serve the soup garnished with parsley.

COOKS' TIPS:

*If fire-roasted canned tomatoes are not available, use plain canned diced tomatoes and add a pinch of hot red pepper flakes.

● For a slightly thicker soup, use a handheld immersion blender to partially purée the vegetables and bologna.

● Feel free to make this soup ahead. It stores exceptionally well in your refrigerator for a day or two, its smoky flavors blending marvelously.

12/14/09 -

used vegetable broth.
forgot garlic, lebanon bologna + pepper, celery seed,
+ Marsala - parsley.   still a very good soup

Really - Potato bean tomato soup.

Mostly-Vegetable Soups

Carrot Soup with Madeira •
Celery-Leek Chowder •
Asparagus Soup •
Cheddar-Butternut Soup •
Broccoli Rice Soup •
Chipotle–Sweet Potato Soup •
Cheddar-Tomato Bisque •
Broccoli Bisque •
Victoria's Brazilian Vegetable Soup •
Classic Potato & Leek Soup •
Broccoli Apple Soup •
Cream of Cauliflower & Parsnip Soup •
Broccoli Vegetarian Soup •
Chunky Cream of Tomato Soup •
with Tarragon
Cabbage Soup with Zucchini •
Cabbage & Beet Soup •
Cauliflower & Roquefort Soup •
Cheese, Potato & Broccoli Soup •
Cream of Potato & Cauliflower Soup •
Cabbage-Carrot Soup •
Creamy Carrot & Potato Soup •
French Onion Soup •
Fresh Tomato-Corn Soup •
Potato-Marsala Soup •
with Herbes de Provence

• Hearty Parsnip-Turnip Soup
• Chunky Potato Leek Soup
• Jalapeño Jack Potato Soup
• Portobello Mushroom Soup
• Chunky Peanut Soup
• Swiss-Potato Soup
• Simple Garlic Soup
• Tomato & Leek Soup
• Thai Coconut Curry Soup
• Ginger Squash Soup
• English Borscht
• Confetti Soup
• Shallot-Watercress Soup
• Chunky Vegetable Soup
• Farmer's Style Tomato Soup
• Ginger Vegetable Soup
• Calabrian Asparagus Soup
• Rich Miso Soup
• Japanese Stock
• German-Style Sour Cream Soup
• Curried Broccoli Soup
• Speedy Cheese Tortellini Soup
• Sorrel Soup
• Spinach-Barley Soup
• Potato & Watercress Soup
• Zucchini Soup Margherita

PREP TIME: 10 MINUTES   COOK TIME: 25 MINUTES

Carrot Soup with Madeira

MAKES 4 SERVINGS

In this tamed version of a fiery Indian soup, curry provides a bit of nip that is balanced by smooth and flavorful Madeira.

2 cans (15 ounces each) reduced-sodium vegetable broth

1 pound carrots, thinly sliced

1 pound potatoes, peeled and cut into 1/2-inch cubes

2 medium onions, chopped

1 teaspoon curry powder

1/2 teaspoon thyme

1 cup low-fat (1%) milk

1/2 cup Madeira

● Combine the broth, carrots, potatoes, onions, curry, and thyme in a 6-quart pot. Cover the pot, and bring the mixture to a boil. Reduce the heat, and simmer until the potatoes and carrots are very tender, 15 to 20 minutes.

● Using a handheld immersion blender, purée the vegetables, stirring in the milk a little at a time. Stir in the Madeira. Warm the soup until it is hot throughout.

COOKS' TIPS:

● A food processor will make short work of chopping the vegetables for this recipe.

● Variation: You may substitute fat-free chicken broth for the vegetable broth and sherry for the Madeira.

PREP TIME: 5 MINUTES   COOK TIME: 25 MINUTES

Celery-Leek Chowder

MAKES 6 SERVINGS

Dressed up with ham and paprika, this creamy chowder gets a light cheese flavor from ricotta.

1 teaspoon olive oil

3 leeks, white parts only, sliced

2 ounces finely diced deli smoked ham

2 large potatoes, peeled and diced

3 cups fat-free beef broth

1 celery stalk, sliced

1 teaspoon white wine vinegar

1/2 teaspoon ground celery seeds

1/4 teaspoon white pepper

1 cup nonfat ricotta cheese

paprika, for garnish

- Warm the oil in a 6-quart pot over medium-high heat for 1 minute. Add the leeks and ham; cook until the leeks are wilted, 3 to 5 minutes.

- Stir in the potatoes, broth, celery, vinegar, celery seeds, and pepper. Cover the pot, and bring the mixture to a boil. Reduce the heat, and simmer for 15 minutes. Stir in the ricotta. Serve garnished with the paprika.

COOKS' TIP:

After stirring in the ricotta, take care not to let the soup boil.

Asparagus Soup

MAKES 6 SERVINGS

Can a soup be light, creamy, elegant, easy, and brimming with asparagus, the harbinger of spring, all at once? Absolutely. Check out this beguiling dish to be sure.

1 pound asparagus

2 teaspoons canola oil

1 medium Spanish onion, chopped

1 medium potato, cut into 1/2-inch cubes

3 cups low-sodium vegetable broth

1/4 teaspoon white pepper

1 cup 2% milk

1/2 teaspoon ground savory

1/4 cup snipped fresh parsley

COOKS' TIP:

The easiest way to remove an asparagus's woody base is to snap it off. If the stalk is tough, remove the outer layer with a vegetable peeler.

- Cut off the asparagus tips. Cut the stalks into 1/2-inch slices, discarding the woody bases. Blanch the tips and stalks for 3 minutes; plunge them into cold water and drain them. Reserve the tips.

- Warm the oil in a 6-quart pot over medium-high heat for 1 minute. Add the onion and sauté until translucent. Stir in the potato, broth, asparagus stalks, and pepper. Cover the pot, and bring the mixture to a boil. Reduce heat, and simmer until potatoes and asparagus are tender, about 12 minutes. Using a hand-held immersion blender, purée the mixture.

- Stir in the milk and savory. Heat until it is hot throughout (do not boil), about 3 minutes. Top each serving with parsley and asparagus tips.

PREP TIME: 10 MINUTES   COOK TIME: 20 MINUTES

Cheddar-Butternut Soup

MAKES 6 SERVINGS

Here's a refreshingly new way to serve butternut squash. A crisp green salad and warm garlic bread are perfect companions to this soup.

2 cans (14 ounces each) fat-free chicken broth

1 butternut squash, peeled and cut into 1-inch cubes

2 potatoes, peeled and cut into 1/2-inch cubes

1 medium onion, chopped

3 cloves garlic, minced

1/4 teaspoon freshly ground black pepper

1/4 teaspoon ground nutmeg

1 cup shredded reduced-fat cheddar cheese

paprika, for garnish

• Combine the broth, squash, potatoes, onion, garlic, pepper, and nutmeg in a 6-quart pot. Cover the pot, and bring the mixture to a boil. Reduce the heat, and simmer until the vegetables are tender, about 15 minutes.

• Remove the pot from the heat. Using a potato masher, mash the squash and potatoes. Stir in the cheddar and serve garnished with the paprika.

COOKS' TIP:

To save time, use 1 pound chopped butternut squash available in your supermarket's produce section.

3/29/08 — handwritten

good light soup — handwritten

Broccoli Rice Soup

MAKES 4 SERVINGS

1 3/4 cups vegetable stock

1 package (10 ounces) frozen broccoli florets,
   thawed, drained, and minced

1/4 cup Minute Rice (uncooked)

1/8 teaspoon ground nutmeg

salt and pepper to taste

● In a 6-quart pot, combine the vegetable stock and broccoli. Bring to a boil, and stir in the rice and nutmeg. Cover tightly, remove from heat, and set aside undisturbed for about 5 minutes.

● Add salt and pepper to taste; serve immediately.

Chipotle–Sweet Potato Soup

as a first course — handwritten

couldn't find chipotles — handwritten

MAKES 4 SERVINGS

The nippy chili- and cumin-laced flavors of the Southwest are among my favorites. Here I've used both to create a captivating soup.

2 cans (14 ounces each) fat-free beef broth

1 large sweet potato, peeled and shredded

1 carrot, shredded

1 medium onion, chopped

1 small chipotle pepper, seeded and chopped

1/2 teaspoon cumin seed

1/4 teaspoon allspice

1/4 teaspoon white pepper

1/2 cup grated reduced-fat Monterey Jack cheese

● Combine the beef broth, sweet potato, carrot, onion, chipotle pepper, cumin, allspice, and white pepper in a 6-quart pot. Cover the pot, and bring the mixture to a boil. Reduce the heat, and simmer for 15 minutes.

● Remove the pot from the heat; using a handheld immersion blender, partially purée the mixture. Stir in the cheese until it melts.

COOKS' TIP:

Chipotles are smoked, dried jalapeño peppers. If you have trouble finding them, substitute a dried cayenne pepper and 1/8 teaspoon mesquite smoke flavoring, which should be added at the end of cooking.

PREP TIME: 10 MINUTES   COOK TIME: 25 MINUTES

Cheddar-Tomato Bisque

MAKES 6 SERVINGS

Here I've taken liberties with the definition of a bisque. This version has a beautiful burnt orange color, the special flavors of tomato and cheddar, and all the usual richness.

1 teaspoon olive oil

1 large onion, chopped

2 cans (14 ounces each) fat-free beef broth

2 large potatoes, peeled and cut into 1/2-inch cubes

4 plum tomatoes, chopped

1 carrot, shredded

2 cloves garlic, crushed

1/4 teaspoon freshly ground black pepper

1/2 teaspoon ground dried savory

1 cup 2% milk

3/4 cup shredded reduced-fat cheddar cheese

1/4 cup snipped fresh parsley, for garnish

● Warm the oil in a 6-quart pot over medium-high heat for 1 minute. Add the onion and sauté until translucent. Stir in the broth, potatoes, tomatoes, carrot, garlic, pepper, and savory. Cover the pot, and bring the mixture to a boil. Reduce the heat, and simmer until the vegetables are tender, about 15 minutes.

● Remove from the heat and, using a handheld immersion blender, purée the mixture. Stir in the milk and cheddar. Reheat until the soup is hot throughout (do not let it boil). Serve garnished with parsley.

COOKS' TIP:

You may subsitute fat-free chicken broth for the beef broth and sage for the savory. Eliminate the carrot and add 1/2 teaspoon sugar.

PREP TIME: 5 MINUTES   COOK TIME: 25 MINUTES

Broccoli Bisque

MAKES 4 SERVINGS

Its cooking time is short, so this soup has plenty of bright and fresh broccoli color and flavor. Nonfat sour cream adds body without fat.

1 can (14 ounces) fat-free chicken broth

1 small potato, finely chopped

1 small onion, finely chopped

1/2 teaspoon reduced-sodium soy sauce

2 cups broccoli florets

1/2 cup nonfat sour cream

1/2 cup 1% milk

1/4 teaspoon fennel seeds, toasted and crushed

● In a 6-quart pot, combine the broth, potato, onion, and soy sauce. Cover the pot, and bring the mixture to a boil. Reduce the heat, and simmer until the potatoes are tender, about 10 minutes.

● Add the broccoli, and simmer the mixture until the broccoli is tender, 5 to 7 minutes. Using a handheld immersion blender, purée the mixture, adding the sour cream, milk, and fennel. Heat the soup until it's hot throughout; do not boil.

COOKS' TIP:

To toast fennel seeds, place them in a small, nonstick skillet. Warm them over medium heat until lightly browned, 3 to 5 minutes, shaking the pan occasionally.

PREP TIME: 10 MINUTES   COOK TIME: 40 MINUTES

Victoria's Brazilian Vegetable Soup

MAKES ABOUT 4 SERVINGS

2 tablespoons vegetable oil

1 medium yellow onion, quartered

3 cloves garlic, chopped

1 serrano chili, stemmed, seeded, and diced

2 large ripe tomatoes, quartered

1 medium carrot, peeled and diced

1 medium sweet potato, peeled and diced

1/2 teaspoon black pepper

10 cups vegetable stock or water

1 can (16 ounces) black beans, rinsed

1 cup finely shredded kale

salt and pepper to taste

3 medium carrots, sliced thin on the diagonal

1/4 cup flat leaf parsley, finely chopped

● Heat the oil in a 6-quart pot, and sauté the onion until lightly colored. Add the garlic and chili pepper and sauté 5 minutes. Add tomatoes, diced carrot, sweet potato, pepper, and vegetable stock. Bring to a boil, reduce to a simmer, partly cover, and cook, stirring occasionally, for about 20 minutes.

● Add the black beans and kale, partly cover, and continue to simmer for about 15 minutes. Remove from heat, and add salt and pepper to taste. Garnish with carrot slices and parsley. Serve immediately.

COOKS' TIP:

You can substitute acorn, butternut, or any other winter squash for the sweet potato.

PREP TIME: 10 MINUTES   COOK TIME: 20 MINUTES

Classic Potato & Leek Soup

MAKES 4 SERVINGS

Seasoned with ham and celery, this popular soup makes for a perfect accompaniment to a special dinner or a speedy supper. It's light. It's easy. It's splendid.

1 teaspoon olive oil

3 leeks, white parts only, sliced

1/4 pound finely diced lean deli ham

3 cups diced potatoes

2 cups fat-free chicken broth

1/2 teaspoon ground celery seeds

1 cup low-fat (1%) milk

1/4 teaspoon freshly ground black pepper

• Warm the oil in a 6-quart pot over medium-high heat for 1 minute. Add the leeks and ham; cook until the leeks are wilted, 3 to 5 minutes.

• Stir in the potatoes, broth, and celery seeds. Cover the pot, and bring the mixture to a boil. Reduce the heat, and simmer for 10 minutes. Stir in the milk and pepper. Cook (do not boil) until the potatoes are tender, 5 to 10 minutes.

COOKS' TIP:

For a light, delicate flavor, take care not to brown the ham and leeks.

PREP TIME: 10 MINUTES   COOK TIME: 40 MINUTES

Broccoli Apple Soup

MAKES 4 SERVINGS

1 tablespoon olive or vegetable oil

2 cups fresh broccoli stems, peeled and diced

3/4 teaspoon crushed dried lemon thyme

1 cup sliced yellow onion

1 McIntosh apple, pared, cored, and diced

1/2 cup diced celery

4 cups vegetable stock or unsweetened apple juice

1/2 cup plumped seedless raisins

salt and pepper to taste

1/4 cup unflavored yogurt or sour cream for garnish

2 tablespoons minced parsley for garnish

COOKS' TIP:

If you use apple juice instead of the vegetable stock, the soup can be served hot or cold.

- Heat the oil in a 6-quart pot, and combine the broccoli, thyme, onion, apple, and celery. Partly cover, and cook, stirring occasionally, until the onion is translucent.

- Add the stock to the vegetables, and bring to a boil. Reduce to a simmer, cover lightly, and cook for about 30 minutes.

- Remove from heat and cool slightly. In the container of a blender or food processor, purée the mixture in batches, until smooth.

- Return the soup to the pot, heat through, and add the raisins and salt and pepper to taste. Serve immediately, garnished with yogurt and parsley.

PREP TIME: 10 MINUTES   COOK TIME: 20 MINUTES

Cream of Cauliflower and Parsnip Soup

MAKES 4 SERVINGS

Thick, satisfying, subtly nutty-tasting, and oh so good. What more could you want from a simple soup that's ready to eat in no time flat?

1 teaspoon olive oil

4 ounces mushrooms, cubed

2 shallots, sliced

2 large potatoes, peeled and cut into 1/2-inch cubes

2 cups cauliflower, broken into florets

1 cup thinly sliced parsnips

2 cups low-sodium vegetable broth

1/2 cup skim milk

1/2 teaspoon dried sage

1/8 teaspoon white pepper

paprika, for garnish

parsley sprigs, for garnish

● Warm the oil in a 6-quart pot over medium-high heat for 1 minute. Add the mushrooms and shallots, and sauté them for 3 minutes.

● Stir in the potatoes, cauliflower, parsnips, and broth. Cover the pot, and bring the mixture to a boil. Reduce the heat, and simmer until the vegetables are tender, about 10 minutes. Using a handheld immersion blender, purée the mixture.

● Stir in the milk, sage, and pepper. Warm the soup until it is hot throughout, about 5 minutes; do not boil. Garnish each serving with the paprika and parsley.

COOKS' TIP:

When puréeing the potatoes and other vegetables, take care not to overwhip them; they may become gummy.

PREP TIME: 15 MINUTES   COOK TIME: 20 MINUTES

Broccoli Vegetarian Soup

MAKES 4 SERVINGS

1 small carrot, peeled and thinly sliced

1 celery stalk and leaves, sliced

1 small white onion, chopped

1 medium clove garlic, minced

1/2 teaspoon crushed dried marjoram

1/4 teaspoon crushed dried basil

1/2 cup vegetable stock

2 cups skim milk

2 cups coarsely chopped broccoli

1/2 cup vegetable-flavored pasta, cooked al dente
  and drained

salt and pepper to taste

ground nutmeg to taste, for garnish

1 cup unflavored yogurt or whipped sour cream,
  for garnish

• In a 6-quart pot, combine the carrot, celery, onion, garlic, marjoram, basil, and stock. Bring to a boil, reduce to a simmer, cover lightly, and cook for about 10 minutes.

• Add the milk and broccoli, and bring to a boil. Reduce heat, cover lightly, and simmer for about 5 minutes, or until the broccoli is tender.

• Remove from heat, and in the container of a blender or food processor, purée the soup, in batches, until smooth.

• Return to the pot, add the pasta, and heat through.

• Turn off the heat, and add salt and pepper to taste. Serve immediately, with the nutmeg and yogurt as a garnish.

PREP TIME: 10 MINUTES   COOK TIME: 20 MINUTES

Chunky Cream of Tomato Soup with Tarragon

MAKES 4 SERVINGS

There are good tomato soups, and there are great tomato soups. This version, with its fresh tomatoes, onions, and tarragon, is among the best. Try it; I'm sure you'll agree.

3 pounds ripe tomatoes

1 teaspoon olive oil

1 large onion, chopped

1 can (14 ounces) fat-free beef broth

1 tablespoon no-salt-added tomato paste

1 tablespoon brown sugar

1/4 teaspoon freshly ground black pepper

1 cup 2% milk

1 teaspoon fresh tarragon leaves

1/2 cup snipped fresh basil leaves

● Peel and seed the tomatoes, reserving the juice. Cut the tomatoes into small chunks.

● Warm the oil in a 6-quart pot over medium-high heat for 1 minute. Add the onion and sauté until golden (do not brown), about 5 minutes. Add the broth, tomatoes and their juice, tomato paste, sugar, and black pepper. Cover the pot, and bring the mixture to a boil. Reduce the heat, and simmer for 10 minutes.

● Stir in the milk and tarragon. Heat the soup until it is hot throughout (do not boil), about 3 minutes. Top each serving with basil.

COOKS' TIPS:

● To peel and seed tomatoes easily, follow these steps:
1. Blanch tomatoes in boiling water for 1 minute and immediately plunge them into icy cold water. Slip off the skins.
2. Cut the tomatoes in half horizontally.
3. Squeeze the halves over a sieve, and discard the seeds.

● To store leftover tomato paste, follow these steps:
1. Coat a small baking sheet with cooking spray.
2. Drop the paste by the tablespoon onto the sheet; place the sheet in the freezer for an hour.
3. Wrap each frozen dollop of paste in waxed paper and place in a freezer bag. Return the paste to the freezer.

PREP TIME: 10 MINUTES   COOK TIME: 25 MINUTES

Cabbage Soup with Zucchini

MAKES 9 SERVINGS

2 tablespoons butter

1 medium yellow onion, sliced

4 medium carrots, peeled and diced

2 1/2 quarts vegetable stock

1 small head cabbage, coarsely chopped

1 cup finely diced zucchini

salt and pepper to taste

• Melt the butter in a 6-quart pot, and sauté the onion until lightly colored.

• Add the carrots and stock, and bring to a boil. Reduce to a simmer, cover lightly, and cook, stirring occasionally, for about 10 minutes. Add the cabbage and zucchini, and cook for about 10 minutes.

• Turn off the heat, and add salt and pepper to taste. Serve immediately.

PREP TIME: 10 MINUTES   COOK TIME: 40 MINUTES

Cabbage & Beet Soup

MAKES 8 SERVINGS

2 cans (16 ounces each) diced tomatoes

1 tablespoon instant vegetable bouillon granules

2 1/2 cups sliced fresh beets

3 medium carrots, peeled and diced

1 large yellow onion, sliced

2 celery stalks with tops, coarsely chopped

water

3 medium cloves garlic, minced

1 medium head cabbage, sliced or cut in wedges

granulated sugar to taste

salt and pepper to taste

2 tablespoons fresh lemon juice

• In a 6-quart pot, combine the tomatoes, bouillon granules, beets, carrots, onion, celery, and enough water to cover them by at least 1 inch. Bring to a boil, reduce to a simmer, cover lightly, and cook for about 20 minutes, or until the vegetables are tender. Add the garlic, cabbage, and sugar. Continue to cook for about 10 minutes.

• Turn off the heat, add salt and pepper to taste, and stir in the lemon juice. Serve immediately.

PREP TIME: 10 MINUTES   COOK TIME: 35 MINUTES

Cauliflower & Roquefort Soup

MAKES 4 SERVINGS

4 tablespoons butter

1 medium onion, chopped

6 cups chopped cauliflower

1 large potato, peeled and diced

1 quart vegetable stock or water

2 tablespoons fresh snipped chives

1/2 teaspoon herbes de Provence

few drops hot pepper sauce

salt and pepper to taste

1 cup heavy cream

2 egg yolks, at room temperature

2 tablespoons brandy or rum

1/2 pound Roquefort cheese

toasted croutons and chives for garnish

• Melt butter in 6-quart pot, and sauté the onion until tender. Tightly cover the pot, turn off the heat, and allow to sit undisturbed for about 10 minutes.

• When ready, adjust the heat under the pot to medium, add the cauliflower and potato, and cook, stirring constantly, for 2 to 3 minutes. Add the stock, chives, herbes de Provence, pepper sauce, and salt and pepper to taste. Bring to a boil. Reduce to a simmer, cover, and cook, stirring occasionally, for about 10 minutes or until the vegetables are tender.

• Remove from heat, and in the container of a blender or food processor, purée in batches. Return to the pot.

• In the container of a blender or food processor, combine the cream, yolks, and brandy and blend until smooth. With the blender running, and pouring in a narrow stream, add 1 cup of the hot soup, and blend until smooth.

• Stir the blended mixture back into the pot, add half the Roquefort, and cook, stirring constantly, until the cheese melts. (Do not allow to boil.) Remove from heat, and serve immediately, garnished with hot toasted croutons, the remaining Roquefort, and chives.

PREP TIME: 10 MINUTES   COOK TIME: 25 MINUTES

Cheese, Potato & Broccoli Soup

MAKES 4 SERVINGS

1/2 cup boiling water

3 tablespoons Herb Ox Vegetable bouillon granules

1 tablespoon butter

1 cup chopped white onions

1 1/3 pounds potatoes, peeled and diced

2 cups water

1 package (10 ounces) frozen broccoli florets, thawed
 and drained

1/2 cup shredded Cheddar or Colby cheese

salt and pepper to taste

- In a cup, combine the 1/2 cup boiling water and bouillon granules. Stir until dissolved. Set aside.

- Melt the butter in a 6-quart pot, and sauté the onions until tender. Add the potatoes, the 2 cups of water, and the bouillon. Bring to a boil. Reduce to a simmer, cover, and cook until the potatoes are tender.

- Using a slotted spoon, remove about 1 cup of potatoes and set aside.

- In the container of a blender or food processor, purée the remaining soup, in batches, until smooth. Return to the pot, and add the reserved potatoes. Stir in the broccoli, and reheat over medium heat (do not allow to boil). Add the cheese, stirring until melted. Remove from heat, add salt and pepper to taste, and serve immediately with a fresh loaf of bread on the side.

11-19-13. Score: 7
Bland. Use sharp cheddar
and fresh broccoli.
May need a spice or two.
Cayenne?

Cream of Potato & Cauliflower Soup

MAKES 4 SERVINGS

Cheddar cheese and cauliflower make a delectable pair, especially in an extra-easy soup like this one.

1 can (14 ounces) low-sodium vegetable broth
1 potato, peeled and cut into 1/2-inch cubes
1/2 pound cauliflower, cut into small florets
1 cup skim milk
1/2 cup shredded Cheddar cheese
1/8 teaspoon white pepper
nutmeg, for garnish

- Pour the broth into a 6-quart pot; add the potato and cauliflower. Cover the pot and bring the mixture to a boil. Reduce the heat; simmer until the vegetables are tender, about 12 minutes.

- Using a slotted spoon, transfer half the vegetables to a bowl; cover with foil to keep them warm. With a handheld immersion blender, purée the vegetables in the pot. Stir in the milk, cheese, white pepper, and reserved vegetables. Cover and heat thoroughly, over a low flame, about 5 minutes. Garnish each serving with nutmeg.

COOKS' TIPS:

- Do not boil the soup after adding the milk, or it might curdle.
- Variation: You may substitute fat-free chicken broth for the vegetable broth and Monterey Jack cheese for the Cheddar cheese.

2/3/08 -
Good - easy - filling
maybe a little bland (Geneva's comment)

PREP TIME: 5 MINUTES COOK TIME: 25 MINUTES

Cabbage-Carrot Soup

MAKES 8 SERVINGS

1 tablespoon butter

1 large clove garlic, chopped

2 celery stalks and leaves, chopped

1 can (16 ounces) red kidney beans, drained

1/2 small head cabbage, chopped

3 medium carrots, peeled and chopped

1 can (28 ounces) diced tomatoes

1 1/2 cups vegetable stock or unsweetened apple juice

salt and pepper to taste

chopped parsley for garnish

● Melt the butter in a 6-quart pot and combine the garlic, celery, beans, cabbage, carrots, tomatoes, and stock. Bring to a boil, reduce to a simmer, cover lightly, and cook, stirring occasionally, for about 20 minutes.

● Remove from heat. Add salt and pepper to taste, and serve in hot bowls with a garnish of parsley.

PREP TIME: 10 MINUTES   COOK TIME: 35 MINUTES

Creamy Carrot & Potato Soup

MAKES 4 SERVINGS

This incredibly thick soup has a warm golden color and tons of flavor, thanks to carrots, onions, thyme, and Canadian bacon.

1 can (14 ounces) fat-free chicken broth

2 large potatoes, peeled and cut into 1/2-inch cubes

1 large carrot, sliced 1/2-inch thick

1/2 teaspoon dried thyme

1/8 teaspoon white pepper

1 onion, chopped

2 ounces Canadian bacon, diced

4 ounces nonfat ricotta cheese

snipped fresh parsley, for garnish

• Combine the broth, potatoes, carrot, thyme, and pepper in a 6-quart pot. Cover the pot, and bring the mixture to a boil. Reduce the heat, and simmer until the potatoes and carrots are tender, 18 to 22 minutes.

• Meanwhile, in a nonstick skillet, cook the onion and bacon until the onion is translucent, about 5 minutes. Remove from heat.

• Using a handheld immersion blender, purée the potatoes and carrot, stirring in the ricotta. Mix in the bacon and onion. Garnish each serving with parsley.

COOKS' TIP:

For a thinner soup, add skim milk or more chicken broth. Heat the soup until it is hot throughout.

PREP TIME: 10 MINUTES   COOK TIME: 30 MINUTES

French Onion Soup

MAKES 4 SERVINGS

In this quick version of the French classic, Madeira wine and Gruyère cheese impart wonderful mellow and nutty flavors. Crisp croutons soak up the tasty broth.

1 teaspoon olive oil

4 medium onions, cut into thin wedges

4 cans fat-free beef broth

1 tablespoon Madeira wine

3 cups plain croutons

1/2 cup shredded Gruyère cheese

1/2 cup snipped fresh parsley

● Warm the oil in a 6-quart pot over medium-high heat for 1 minute. Add the onions, and sauté until they're golden, about 8 minutes. Add the broth. Cover the pot, and bring the mixture to a boil. Reduce the heat, and simmer for 15 minutes. Stir in the Madeira.

● Divide the croutons among 4 soup bowls. Ladle in the soup, top each serving with cheese, and place under the broiler for 3 to 4 minutes, or until bubbling. Garnish with parsley.

COOKS' TIP:

To make croutons, cut white or whole wheat bread into 3/4-inch cubes. Spread the cubes on a baking sheet and mist them with cooking spray. Broil until they're golden, about 3 minutes. Shake the pan or stir the cubes to expose the untoasted sides. Mist with cooking oil spray and broil another 2 to 3 minutes.

11/27/2013
Lots of vegetables
Jim 6 1/2
Beth 7 1/2

PREP TIME: 10 MINUTES   COOK TIME: 15 MINUTES

Fresh Tomato-Corn Soup

MAKES 4 SERVINGS

In summer, when fresh vegetables and herbs are at their peak, create a sensation with this lively vegetarian soup. It comes together in a snap and takes less than 15 minutes to cook.

2 teaspoons olive oil

1 cup chopped red onion

4 cloves garlic, minced

1 can (14 ounces) low-sodium vegetable broth

2 cups diced zucchini

1 pound fresh tomatoes, chopped

1 1/2 cups frozen corn

1/2 teaspoon crushed red pepper flakes

1/4 cup snipped fresh basil leaves

2 tablespoons bacon bits, for garnish

· added parmesan as garnish

● Warm the oil in a 6-quart pot over medium-high heat for 1 minute. Add the onion and garlic, and sauté until the onion is translucent, about 3 minutes.

● Stir in the broth, zucchini, tomatoes, corn, and red pepper flakes. Cover the pot, and bring the mixture to a boil. Reduce the heat, and simmer until the zucchini is tender, about 10 minutes.

● Stir in the basil. Top each serving with bacon bits.

COOKS' TIP:

Keep the cooking time short so the tomatoes and zucchini retain their fresh flavors.

PREP TIME: 10 MINUTES   COOK TIME: 20 MINUTES

Potato-Marsala Soup with Herbes de Provence

MAKES 4 SERVINGS

This uncommonly delicious soup gives a whole new meaning to fast food. Prosciutto adds panache while roasted red peppers lend color.

2¹/2 cups fat-free chicken broth

3 cups diced peeled potatoes

1 large onion, chopped

1 celery stalk, chopped

¹/2 cup Marsala wine

2 ounces prosciutto, chopped

¹/2 teaspoon herbes de Provence

¹/4 cup diced roasted red peppers

- Combine the broth, potatoes, onion, celery, wine, prosciutto, and herbs in a 6-quart pot. Cover the pot, and bring the mixture to a boil. Reduce the heat, and simmer until the potatoes are tender, 12 to 15 minutes.

- Using a handheld immersion blender, process the mixture until it is partially puréed. Top each serving with the roasted peppers.

COOKS' TIP:

Herbes de Provence is a commercial blend of dried herbs that's typical of the cuisine of southern France. If you can't find it in your supermarket, substitute a pinch each of rosemary, marjoram, thyme, and sage.

PREP TIME: 15 MINUTES   COOK TIME: 20 MINUTES

Hearty Parsnip-Turnip Soup

MAKES 4 SERVINGS

Because their cooking time is short, the root veggies in this soup—parsnips, carrots, and turnips—taste flavorful yet mild. Dill and thyme provide just the right seasoning.

2 cans (14 ounces each) fat-free chicken broth

1 parsnip, diced

1 turnip, diced

1 yellow summer squash, diced

1 carrot, diced

1 potato, peeled and diced

1 onion, chopped

1/2 teaspoon fresh thyme leaves

1/4 teaspoon freshly ground black pepper

1/4 teaspoon dried dill weed

1/4 teaspoon paprika, for garnish

• Combine the broth, parsnip, turnip, squash, carrot, potato, onion, thyme, pepper, and dill weed in a 6-quart pot. Cover the pot, and bring the mixture to a boil. Reduce the heat, and simmer until the vegetables are tender, about 12 minutes. Transfer half the vegetables to a bowl; cover with foil to keep them warm.

• Using a handheld immersion blender, purée the vegetables remaining in the pot. Return the reserved vegetables to the pot. Serve garnished with paprika.

11/22   8 pts.
Flavorful, somewhat hardy
cooked on stove rather
than microwave.

MOSTLY-VEGETABLE SOUPS

PREP TIME: 5 MINUTES   COOK TIME: 15 MINUTES

Chunky Potato Leek Soup

MAKES 4 SERVINGS

2 teaspoons butter

1 cup sliced leeks

2 cups vegetable stock

2 cups cubed potatoes

1 cup canned whole-kernel corn

2 tablespoons fresh dill weed, chopped

2 teaspoons grated Parmesan cheese

red pepper sauce to taste

salt and pepper

• In a 2-quart microwave-safe casserole, combine the butter and leeks, and microwave on high, stirring once, for about 3 minutes. Add the stock and potatoes, cover lightly with a vented cover, and microwave, stirring twice, on high for about 4 minutes.

• Add the corn, dill, cheese, and pepper sauce. Once more, cover with the vented cover, and cook on high for about 4 minutes, or until the potatoes are tender.

• Add salt and pepper to taste, and set aside for 2 to 3 minutes before serving.

PREP TIME: 10 MINUTES   COOK TIME: 25 MINUTES

Jalapeño Jack Potato Soup

MAKES 4 SERVINGS

I just love the way cheese and ordinary potatoes create a yummy soup to die for! For crunch, serve this soup with crudités, croutons, or crusty French bread.

6 large or 10 medium potatoes, peeled and cut into $1/2$-inch cubes

1 can (14 ounces) fat-free chicken broth

1 medium onion, finely chopped

$1/2$ teaspoon celery seeds

1 cup skim milk

1 cup shredded jalapeño Monterey Jack cheese

caraway seeds, for garnish

• Combine the potatoes, broth, onion, and celery seeds in a 6-quart pot. Cover the pot, and bring the mixture to a boil. Reduce the heat, and simmer until the potatoes are tender, 15 to 20 minutes.

• Using a potato masher or handheld immersion blender, mash the potatoes, stirring in the milk a little at a time. Mix in the cheese and cook until it has melted, about 5 minutes. Garnish each serving with the caraway seeds.

COOKS' TIP:

To make this soup still lower in fat, you can use a fat-free cheese, such as fat-free cheddar or Swiss. Just be aware that the flavor and texture will be different.

PREP TIME: 10 MINUTES   COOK TIME: 25 MINUTES

Portobello Mushroom Soup

MAKES 4 SERVINGS

For mushroom aficionados, here's a splendid soup that's thick and dark, with loads of substantial portobello mushrooms. For mellowness, I've added a splash of dry sherry, and for bright color, I've topped each serving with snipped chives.

2 teaspoons butter

6 ounces small portobello mushrooms, sliced

1 large onion, chopped

2 cups fat-free chicken broth

1 large potato, peeled and shredded

2 bay leaves

1/4 teaspoon white pepper

1 cup 2% milk

1 tablespoon dry sherry

1/4 cup snipped fresh chives

4 attractive mushroom slices for a garnish

- Melt the butter in a 6-quart pot over medium-high heat. Add the mushrooms and onion, and sauté until the onion is translucent. Stir in the broth, potato, and bay leaves. Cover the pot, and bring the mixture to a boil. Reduce the heat, and simmer for 15 minutes. Discard the bay leaves. Stir in the pepper.

- Using a handheld immersion blender, purée the mixture. Stir in the milk and sherry. Heat the soup until it is hot throughout (do not boil), about 5 minutes. Top each serving with chives and mushroom slices.

COOKS' TIP:

To clean mushrooms, wipe them with a damp paper towel or rinse them quickly under cool running water. Never soak mushrooms; their flavor will be lost.

PREP TIME: 20 MINUTES   COOK TIME: 35 MINUTES

Chunky Peanut Soup

MAKES 8 SERVINGS

2 tablespoons butter

1 medium yellow onion, diced

2 medium carrots, peeled and diced

8 cups vegetable stock

1 cup crunchy peanut butter

1 small fresh ripe tomato, quartered

4 small potatoes, peeled and diced

1 small green pepper, roasted, peeled, seeded,
    and diced

3 tablespoons minced fresh parsley

1 large (about 3 pounds) zucchini, diced

2 cans (8 ounces) sliced button mushrooms, drained

3 tablespoons freshly squeezed lemon juice

salt and cayenne pepper to taste

• Melt the butter in a 6-quart pot, and sauté the onion until just tender. Add the carrots, and continue to cook, stirring occasionally, for about 5 minutes.

• Meanwhile, in a bowl, beat 1 cup of the stock with the peanut butter using a wire whisk, until smooth.

• Add the remaining stock, tomato, potatoes, green pepper, and 2 tablespoons of the parsley to the pot. Bring to a boil, add the peanut butter mixture, and return to a boil. Reduce to a simmer, partly cover, and cook for about 15 minutes, or until the potatoes are fork tender. Add the zucchini and mushrooms, and cook, stirring, until the zucchini is tender.

• Turn off the heat, and add the lemon juice and add salt and pepper to taste. Ladle into soup bowls and sprinkle with the remaining parsley just before serving.

PREP TIME: 10 MINUTES   COOK TIME: 20 MINUTES

Swiss Potato Soup

MAKES 4 SERVINGS

A rich-tasting soup like this one needn't be reserved for special occasions. Why? It's rich in cheese flavor, not calories and fat, and it's ready to eat in 30 minutes or less.

1 teaspoon olive oil

1 large onion, chopped

1 can (14 ounces) fat-free chicken broth

2 large potatoes, peeled and cut into 1/2-inch cubes

1 celery stalk, chopped

1/8 teaspoon white pepper

1/2 teaspoon dried thyme leaves

1 cup skim milk

3/4 cup shredded reduced-fat Swiss cheese

1/4 cup snipped fresh chives, for garnish

● Warm the oil in a 6-quart pot over medium-high heat for 1 minute. Add the onion and sauté until translucent. Stir in the broth, potatoes, celery, pepper, and thyme. Cover the pot, and bring the mixture to a boil. Reduce the heat, and simmer until the potatoes are tender, about 10 minutes.

● Remove from the heat, and mash the mixture with a potato masher. Stir in the milk, and return the mixture to the heat. Stir in the cheese; cook until it melts, stirring constantly. Serve garnished with chives.

COOKS' TIP:

If you can't find fresh chives, use the frozen or dried variety.

PREP TIME: 10 MINUTES   COOK TIME: 25 MINUTES

Simple Garlic Soup

MAKES 4 SERVINGS

Don't be intimidated by the amount of garlic in this recipe. Gentle cooking tames garlic's flavor and makes it mild, almost sweet.

1 teaspoon olive oil

1 head garlic, cloves peeled and sliced

2 cans (14 ounces each) fat-free chicken broth

1 tablespoon snipped fresh fennel leaves

1 tablespoon dry sherry

2 cups whole wheat croutons

1/4 cup snipped fresh parsley

- Warm the oil in a 6-quart pot over medium-high heat for 1 minute. Add the garlic, and sauté until golden (do not brown), 3 to 5 minutes, stirring constantly. Add the broth and fennel; simmer the mixture for 15 minutes. Stir in the sherry.

- Top each serving with croutons and parsley.

COOKS' TIP:

See the Cooks' Tip under French Onion Soup, page 130, for directions on making croutons.

PREP TIME: 5 MINUTES   COOK TIME: 40 MINUTES

Tomato & Leek Soup

MAKES 8 SERVINGS

Here's a marvelous tomato soup that's really low in calories and fat. Beef broth and a measure of sherry are the secret flavor ingredients.

1 teaspoon olive oil

2 large leeks, white parts only, thinly sliced

2 celery stalks, thinly sliced

2 cans (14 ounces each) fat-free beef broth

1 can (28 ounces) whole plum tomatoes, cut up

1 tablespoon brown sugar

1/4 teaspoon lemon pepper

2 tablespoons dry sherry

2 bay leaves

2 teaspoons dried dill weed

● Warm the oil in a 6-quart pot over medium-high heat for 1 minute. Add the leeks and celery, and sauté until the leeks are translucent and the celery is tender, about 5 minutes. Stir in the broth, tomatoes, sugar, pepper, sherry, and bay leaves.

● Cover the pot and bring the mixture to a boil. Reduce the heat, and simmer the soup for 30 minutes. Discard the bay leaves. Stir in the dill.

COOKS' TIPS:

● Have some fresh dill on hand? (Maybe it'll bring good luck; the ancient Romans thought it would.) Garnish each serving with a small sprig—along with a slice of lemon.
● For a vegetarian soup, substitute vegetable broth for the beef variety.
● Prefer a silky smooth tomato soup? After discarding the bay leaves, purée the soup, in batches, in a blender.

PREP TIME: 10 MINUTES   COOK TIME: 25 MINUTES

Thai Coconut Curry Soup

MAKES 4 SERVINGS

2 teaspoons coconut milk

2 cups unsweetened apple juice or vegetable stock

1 stalk lemon grass, cut into 1-inch lengths

4-inch piece fresh gingerroot, peeled and
   thinly sliced

1 tablespoon curry powder

1/2 teaspoon turmeric

2 teaspoons grated lime zest

2 tablespoons fresh lime juice

2 teaspoons Chinese-style chili sauce

1 tablespoon sesame oil

8 white button mushrooms, trimmed

1/4 pound soba noodles or thin spaghetti, cooked
   al dente

salt and pepper to taste

cilantro sprigs for garnish

● In a 6-quart pot, combine the coconut milk, apple juice, lemon grass, ginger, curry, turmeric, lime zest and juice, and chili sauce. Bring to a boil. Reduce to a simmer, cover lightly, and cook, stirring occasionally, for about 20 minutes.

● Add the oil, mushrooms, and noodles to the hot soup.

● Turn off the heat, and add salt and pepper to taste. Serve immediately, with cilantro sprigs as a garnish.

COOKS' TIP:

Soba noodles and Chinese chili sauce can be found in Asian food stores or very large supermarkets.

PREP TIME: 20 MINUTES   COOK TIME: 20 MINUTES

Ginger Squash Soup

MAKES 6 SERVINGS

2 tablespoons butter

1 large yellow onion, chopped

1 small clove garlic, chopped

2 teaspoons grated fresh gingerroot

2 tablespoons all-purpose flour

1 1/2 cups vegetable stock

2 cups cooked summer squash

2 teaspoons grated orange zest

1/2 cup fresh orange juice

salt and pepper to taste

1/4 teaspoon ground nutmeg

fresh chopped parsley

COOKS' TIP:

Ginger and garlic bring alive the flavor of the squash, which might otherwise remain bland.

- In a 2-quart microwave-proof casserole, combine the butter, onion, garlic, and gingerroot and microwave on high, stirring once, for 4 to 5 minutes, or until the onion is tender.

- Blend the flour with the stock, and add to the casserole dish. Also add the squash, and microwave on high, stirring once, for 7 to 9 minutes, or until the liquid is boiling and thickened.

- In the container of a blender or food processor, purée the soup, in batches, until smooth. Add the orange zest and juice, and process until incorporated.

- Return to the casserole, add salt and pepper to taste, and stir in the nutmeg. Microwave on high for about 2 minutes. Ladle into heated bowls. Sprinkle with parsley and serve immediately.

PREP TIME: 10 MINUTES   COOK TIME: 1 HOUR 10 MINUTES

English Borscht

MAKES 4 SERVINGS

1¹/2 cups peeled and grated fresh beets

1¹/2 cups finely shredded red cabbage

3 tablespoons tomato paste

2 tablespoons red wine vinegar

3 tablespoons butter or margarine

4 cups vegetable or chicken stock

1 large red onion, minced

1 large carrot, peeled and grated

salt and pepper to taste

1 tablespoon molasses

whipped sour cream or unflavored yogurt for garnish

● In a large saucepan, combine the beets, cabbage, tomato paste, vinegar, 1¹/2 tablespoons of the butter, and stock. Bring to a boil. Reduce to a simmer, cover, and cook, stirring occasionally, for 55 to 60 minutes, or until the beets are very tender.

● Melt the remaining butter in a skillet, and sauté the onion and carrot together until the onion is browned. Transfer to the saucepan, and continue to cook for 10 to 12 minutes. Add salt and pepper to taste, stir in the molasses, and serve with a garnish of sour cream.

Confetti Soup

MAKES 12 SERVINGS

You will know why this soup is called Confetti when you see the multitude of bright colors in your soup bowls!

1 tablespoon canola oil

2 medium yellow onions, minced

4 large carrots, peeled and diced

2 large fennel bulbs, diced

10 cups vegetable stock or water

1 teaspoon crushed dried tarragon

1 teaspoon crushed dried thyme

1 large red bell pepper, stemmed, seeded, and diced

2 medium zucchini, peeled and diced

12 large fresh mushrooms, quartered

salt and pepper to taste

grated Parmesan cheese for garnish

- Heat the oil in 6-quart pot, and sauté the onions, cooking until soft. Add the carrots, fennel, stock, tarragon, and thyme. Bring to a boil, reduce to a simmer, partially cover, and cook, stirring occasionally, for about 20 minutes, or until the vegetables are tender.

- Add the red bell pepper, zucchini, and mushrooms. Cover lightly, and cook for about 10 minutes.

- Turn off the heat, and add salt and pepper to taste. Serve immediately with Parmesan cheese on top.

PREP TIME: 10 MINUTES   COOK TIME: 25 MINUTES

Shallot-Watercress Soup

MAKES 4 SERVINGS

Six ingredients—that's all it takes to make this sensational soup, which showcases piquant shallots and watercress. In each spoonful, a caper or two provide an intriguing burst of flavor.

2 teaspoons butter
8 shallots, thinly sliced
1 medium potato, finely chopped
2 cans (14 ounces each) fat-free chicken broth
1/2 bunch (about 2 ounces) watercress, leaves only
2 teaspoons capers, rinsed and drained

● Melt the butter in a 6-quart pot over medium-high heat. Add the shallots, and cook them until they are translucent, about 3 minutes. Add the potato and 3/4 cup broth, and cook until the potatoes are tender, about 10 minutes.

● Using a handheld immersion blender, purée the mixture. Stir in the remaining broth, and heat the soup until it is hot throughout, 3 to 5 minutes. Stir in the watercress, and heat for 1 minute more. Add the capers and serve immediately.

PREP TIME: 10 MINUTES   COOK TIME: 15 MINUTES

Chunky Vegetable Soup

MAKES 4 SERVINGS

Asparagus spears were once called the arrows of the gods, and they add a lot to vegetable soup.

1 1/2 cups water

4 scallions

3 asparagus spears

1 medium (about 1 1/2 pounds) zucchini, quartered
    lengthwise

1 broccoli stalk, peeled and quartered lengthwise

1/4 cup butter

1 medium yellow onion, minced

1 celery stalk, minced

2 tablespoons all-purpose flour

1 1/4 cups milk

salt and pepper to taste

• Put the water in the base of a steamer, and bring to a boil. In the upper section of the steamer, combine the scallions, asparagus, zucchini, and broccoli. Cover and steam for 5 to 7 minutes, or until the vegetables are tender.

• Reserve the liquid from the base of the steamer. Transfer the vegetables to a platter. When they are cool to the touch, dice and set them aside.

• Melt the butter in a large saucepan, and sauté the onion and celery until tender. Sprinkle in the flour, stirring until incorporated. Pouring in a narrow stream and stirring constantly, add the milk and reserved liquid. Bring to a boil, stir in the steamed vegetables, heat through, and add salt and pepper to taste. Serve immediately.

Farmer's Style Tomato Soup

MAKES 6 SERVINGS

1/4 cup plus 2 tablespoons extra virgin olive oil

2 medium yellow onions, coarsely chopped

3 medium cloves garlic, minced

2 celery stalks, chopped

3 cans (16 ounces each) diced tomatoes

3 pieces day-old Italian bread, crusts removed

4 cups hot vegetable stock

1/2 cup chopped fresh basil leaves

2 tablespoons chopped fresh parsley

2 tablespoons chopped fresh marjoram

salt and pepper to taste

● Heat the oil in a 6-quart pot, and sauté the onions, garlic, and celery together until the onions are tender. Reduce the heat to low, add the tomatoes, cover lightly, and cook for about 10 minutes.

● Place the bread in a bowl, and pour 1 cup of hot stock over the top. Using the back of a spoon, mash the bread until blended with the stock.

● Stir the softened bread and remaining stock into the tomatoes, and cook, stirring frequently, for about 30 minutes.

● Add the basil, parsley, and marjoram during the last 5 minutes of cooking time. Remove from heat, and in the container of a blender or food processor, purée the soup, in batches, until smooth. Return to the pot and heat through.

● Turn off the heat, and add salt and pepper to taste. Serve immediately.

PREP TIME: 15 MINUTES   COOK TIME: 30 MINUTES

Ginger Vegetable Soup

MAKES 4 SERVINGS

1 medium yellow onion, sliced

1 stalk celery, thinly sliced

1 green bell pepper, seeded and sliced

1/4 teaspoon crushed garlic

2 teaspoons minced fresh gingerroot

1/2 cup water

4 cups vegetable stock

1 can (8 ounces) tomato sauce

2 white potatoes, peeled and diced

1 teaspoon crushed dried basil

1 teaspoon paprika

1/3 teaspoon ground black pepper

1 small zucchini, halved lengthwise and sliced

2 cups frozen whole corn kernels

salt and pepper to taste

• In a 6-quart pot, combine the onion, celery, green pepper, garlic, and gingerroot. Add the water, bring to a boil, and cook for about 5 minutes, or until the celery is tender.

• Add the stock, tomato sauce, potatoes, basil, paprika, pepper, zucchini, and corn. Return to a boil, cover lightly, and cook, stirring occasionally, until the potatoes are tender. Remove from heat, add salt and black pepper to taste, and serve immediately.

PREP TIME: 5 MINUTES   COOK TIME: 30 MINUTES

Calabrian Asparagus Soup

MAKES 6 SERVINGS

Calabria is a region in southern Italy renowned for culinary achievements—and this soup can certainly be counted as one.

2 tablespoons virgin olive oil
2 medium cloves garlic, minced
2 pounds fresh asparagus, cut into 1-inch pieces
4 cups vegetable stock
4 large eggs, beaten
1/2 cup freshly grated Romano or Parmesan cheese
6 slices Italian bread, toasted, for serving

● Heat the oil in a 6-quart pot, and sauté the garlic until golden. Add the asparagus and cook, stirring constantly, until tender. Add the stock, and bring to a boil. Reduce to a simmer and cook for about 15 minutes.

● Meanwhile in a bowl, beat the eggs until foamy, and then beat in the cheese. Beating constantly and adding a few spoonfuls at a time, add about 2 cups of the hot liquid.

● Blend the egg mixture into the soup, stirring constantly. Continue to cook, stirring frequently, until liquid is just thickened. Remove from heat.

● In each serving bowl, place one slice of bread and ladle the soup over the top. Serve immediately.

PREP TIME: 10 MINUTES   COOK TIME: 40 MINUTES

Rich Miso Soup

MAKES 6 SERVINGS

2 tablespoons virgin olive oil
4 medium yellow onions, finely minced
2 large cloves garlic, minced
1 1/2 cups finely diced potatoes
1/2 cup diced carrots
1 teaspoon ground cumin
1 tablespoon tamari or soy sauce
4 cups Japanese Stock (see page 155)
1 heaping tablespoon dark brown miso

● Heat the oil in a saucepan, and sauté the onions and garlic together until translucent. Add the potatoes and carrots, and heat through. Add the cumin, tamari, and stock. Bring to a boil. Reduce to a simmer, cover tightly, and cook, stirring occasionally, for about 30 minutes, or until the vegetables are fork tender.

● Remove from heat, add the miso, and using a blender or food processor, purée in batches until smooth. Return to the stove, heat through, and serve immediately, with a salt-free cracker on the side.

COOKS' TIP:

Miso, a soybean paste popular in Japan, is available in Asian markets and in very large supermarkets. It can usually be found in three varieties. Yellow is the saltiest and dark brown is the most palatable.

PREP TIME: 10 MINUTES COOK TIME: 40 MINUTES

Japanese Stock

MAKES 6 CUPS

2 *tablespoons extra virgin olive oil*

4 *medium white onions, sliced*

9 *medium cloves garlic, chopped*

3 *medium carrots, peeled and chopped*

2 *sprigs fresh thyme*

1/4 *teaspoon ground cumin*

4 *teaspoons tamari or soy sauce*

6 *cups water*

● Heat the oil in a saucepan, and sauté the onions and garlic until translucent. Add the carrots, thyme, cumin, tamari, and water. Bring to a boil, reduce to a simmer, cover tightly, and cook for about 30 minutes.

● Remove from heat, and use a blender or food processor to purée the mixture in batches until smooth. Strain it through a very fine sieve into the saucepan, discarding the vegetable matter, and use as desired.

COOKS' TIP:

Make this stock ahead of time and keep it in the freezer until needed.

PREP TIME: 15 MINUTES   COOK TIME: 2 HOURS

German-Style Sour Cream Soup

MAKES 6 SERVINGS

2 tablespoons canola oil

3/4 cup chopped cabbage

1/2 cup chopped onion

1/2 cup chopped celery

1/2 cup chopped carrots

3/4 cup diced turnips

3/4 cup diced acorn squash

4 cups diced tomatoes

4 cups vegetable stock

1/4 cup quick-cooking barley

1/4 cup pearl rice

1/2 cup vinegar

1 clove garlic, minced

1 teaspoon caraway seeds

2 teaspoons Worcestershire sauce

1/4 teaspoon dried thyme

salt and pepper to taste

1 cup sour cream or unflavored yogurt

● Heat the oil in a 6-quart pot, and sauté the cabbage, onion, celery, carrots, turnips, and squash until the onion is translucent. Cover tightly and cook on a low heat for about 15 minutes, or until the turnips are fork tender. Add the tomatoes, stock, barley, and rice. Cover tightly, and continue to cook for about 90 minutes.

● In a bowl, blend the vinegar, garlic, caraway seeds, Worcestershire sauce, and thyme. Stir into the soup mixture, and bring to a boil. Then reduce to a simmer, cover again, and cook, stirring occasionally, for about 10 minutes.

● Turn off the heat, and add salt and pepper to taste. Serve immediately with the sour cream on the side.

PREP TIME: 5 MINUTES   COOK TIME: 40 MINUTES

Curried Broccoli Soup

MAKES 6 SERVINGS

2 tablespoons butter

1 cup chopped yellow onion

1/2 cup chopped green bell pepper

1 medium clove garlic, minced

1/2 teaspoon ginger powder

1/2 teaspoon curry powder

1/4 teaspoon turmeric powder

1 3/4 cups vegetable stock

1/2 cup water

2 packages (10 ounces each) frozen chopped
   broccoli, thawed and drained

1/2 to 3/4 cup half-and-half

salt and white pepper to taste

• Melt the butter in a 6-quart pot, and sauté the onion, pepper, and garlic together until the onion is translucent. Sprinkle in the ginger, curry powder, and turmeric, and continue to cook, stirring constantly, for about 1 minute. Add the stock, water, and broccoli. Bring to a boil, reduce to a simmer, and cover lightly. Cook, stirring occasionally, for about 30 minutes, or until the broccoli is tender.

• In the container of a blender or food processor, purée the soup, in batches, until smooth.

• Return to the pot, and add enough half-and-half to achieve the desired consistency.

• Turn off the heat, and add salt and pepper to taste. Serve immediately.

PREP TIME: 5 MINUTES   COOK TIME: 10 MINUTES

Speedy Cheese Tortellini Soup

MAKES 6 SERVINGS

Need dinner on the double? Then you've opened to the right recipe. This easy soup takes just 10 minutes to cook, and it's packed with tomatoes, cheese tortellini, sweet peppers, and scallions.

2 cups coarsely chopped tomatoes

2 cans (14 ounces each) fat-free chicken broth

1/2 cup sliced scallions (about 3)

1/2 cup chopped red or green sweet peppers

1 teaspoon Italian herb seasoning

1/8 teaspoon celery seeds

1/4 teaspoon crushed red pepper flakes

2 cups (about 1 pound) frozen tricolor cheese
   tortellini

1 tablespoon snipped fresh basil

● Combine the tomatoes, broth, scallions, peppers, herb seasoning, celery seeds, and pepper flakes in a 6-quart pot. Cover the pot, and bring the mixture to a boil. Stir in the tortellini, and simmer the soup until the tortellini are al dente, about 10 minutes. Stir in the basil, and serve immediately.

COOKS' TIPS:

● Because tortellini become soggy when stored in broth, serve this soup freshly made.
● Variations: You may substitute fat-free beef broth for the chicken broth and sausage tortellini for the cheese variety. Small ravioli may be used instead of the tortellini.

Sorrel Soup

MAKES 4 SERVINGS

3$1/2$ tablespoons butter

3 tablespoons all-purpose flour

1$1/2$ quarts vegetable stock

1 bunch fresh French sorrel

1 bunch fresh chervil

1 egg yolk

$1/2$ teaspoon granulated sugar

salt and pepper to taste

4 to 5 tablespoons sour cream or unflavored yogurt

finely minced garlic for garnish

• Melt the butter in a 6-quart pot and sprinkle in the flour, stirring to make a roux. Stir in the stock, sorrel, and chervil, and bring to a boil.

• Meanwhile, in a bowl, use a wire whisk to beat the egg yolk until foamy. Beat in $1/4$ cup of hot soup. Stir yolk mixture back into the soup. Cook, stirring constantly, until thickened. Do not boil.

• Turn off the heat, stir in the sugar, salt and pepper to taste, and sour cream. Serve immediately, with a sprinkling of minced garlic on top.

COOKS' TIP:

This recipe calls for French sorrel, which has less acid content than wild sorrel.

Spinach-Barley Soup

MAKES 2 TO 3 SERVINGS

2*1/2 cups vegetable stock or water*

1 package (10 ounces) creamed spinach, drained

1/4 cup quick-cooking barley

1/8 teaspoon ground nutmeg

salt and pepper to taste

● In a 6-quart pot combine the stock and spinach. Bring to a boil, stir in the barley and nutmeg, and reduce to a simmer. Cover lightly and cook, stirring frequently, 15 minutes or until the barley is tender.

● Turn off the heat, add the salt and pepper to taste, and set aside for about 5 minutes. Serve immediately.

PREP TIME: 5 MINUTES   COOK TIME: 30 MINUTES

Potato & Watercress Soup

MAKES 4 SERVINGS

4 potatoes, peeled and diced

4 cups cold water

1 bunch fresh watercress, chopped

1 tablespoon butter

1/2 cup milk

salt and pepper to taste

COOKS' TIP:

For variations, substitute unsweetened apple juice or vegetable stock for the water. To create a rich, thick soup, use heavy cream instead of milk.

● In a 6-quart pot, combine the potatoes and water, bring to a boil, and cook for about 20 minutes, or until the potatoes are fork tender.

● With a slotted spoon, remove the potatoes and press through a fine sieve. Return them to the pot, add the watercress, and bring to a slow boil. Reduce to a simmer, and cook for about 5 minutes. Add the butter and milk. Heat through.

● Turn off the heat, and add salt and pepper to taste. Serve immediately.

PREP TIME: 10 MINUTES   COOK TIME: 20 MINUTES

Zucchini Soup Margherita

MAKES 4 SERVINGS

Refreshing and light, this soup, which is brimming with mozzarella and basil, takes its name from a pizza specialty of Naples, Italy. According to legend, the cheese pizza, with the colors of the Italian flag, was created to honor a Queen—Margherita. For a special twist, try adding cooked green beans and celery.

2 teaspoons olive oil

8 ounces small zucchini, halved lengthwise
   and sliced

1 medium onion, chopped

4 cloves garlic, chopped

2 cans (14 ounces each) fat-free chicken broth

8 ounces plum tomatoes, sliced

1/4 teaspoon freshly ground black pepper

1 teaspoon balsamic vinegar

1/2 cup shredded part-skim mozzarella cheese,
   for garnish

1/2 cup snipped fresh basil, for garnish

• Warm the oil in a 6-quart pot over medium-high heat for 1 minute. Add the zucchini, onion, and garlic, and sauté until the vegetables start to brown, 3 to 5 minutes. Stir in the broth, tomatoes, pepper, and vinegar.

• Cover the pot, and bring the mixture to a boil. Reduce the heat, and simmer for 10 minutes. Serve garnished with the mozzarella and basil.

Catch-of-the-Day Soups

PREP TIME: 5 MINUTES   COOK TIME: 25 MINUTES

Crab Bisque

MAKES 4 SERVINGS

This delightful soup is elegant enough for a special dinner, easy enough for a casual supper, and fast enough to prepare anytime you wish.

butter-flavored cooking spray
1 medium onion, minced
1 can (10 ounces) clam juice
1 carrot, finely chopped
1 large potato, peeled and finely chopped
1 can (6³/4 ounces) flaked crabmeat
4 tablespoons fat-free cream cheese
¹/8 teaspoon mace
1¹/2 cups 2% milk
1 tablespoon sherry
¹/4 teaspoon paprika
¹/8 teaspoon white pepper

● Coat the bottom of a 3-quart saucepan with cooking spray. Add the onion, and cook over medium-high heat until translucent, about 3 minutes.

● Stir in the clam juice, carrot, and potato. Cover the pan and simmer the mixture until the vegetables are tender, about 10 minutes. Stir in the crabmeat, cream cheese, and mace. Using a handheld immersion blender, purée the mixture until smooth.

● Stir in the milk, and heat over a low flame until the mixture is hot, 5 to 10 minutes. Stir in the sherry, paprika, and pepper; serve immediately.

COOKS' TIP:

Cutting the potato and carrot into very small pieces, or even coarsely shredding them, will speed cooking.

Thai Curry Noodle Soup

MAKES 4 SERVINGS

2 tablespoons canola oil

3 medium cloves garlic, chopped

1 tablespoon red curry paste

1/2 cup thick coconut cream

1/2 cup coconut milk

2 1/2 cups vegetable stock

2 teaspoons curry powder

1/4 teaspoon turmeric powder

3 tablespoons Thai fish sauce (nam pla)
   (optional)

1 teaspoon granulated sugar

1 cup shredded cabbage

1 1/2 teaspoons lemon juice

1 pound Chinese-style thin noodles, cooked,
   drained, and rinsed

2 scallions, coarsely chopped, for garnish

2 lemons, cut into wedges, for garnish

● Heat the oil in a saucepan, and sauté the garlic until lightly colored. Add the curry paste, heat through, and add the coconut cream; stir continuously until oily. Add the coconut milk, stock, curry powder, turmeric, fish sauce, and sugar. Continue to cook, stirring for 4 to 5 minutes. Add the cabbage, stirring briefly to incorporate. Remove from heat, and stir in the lemon juice.

● Divide the cooked noodles among 4 soup bowls, and ladle the hot soup over the top. Garnish with scallions, and serve immediately with lemon wedges on the side.

PREP TIME: 10 MINUTES   COOK TIME: 30 MINUTES

Provençale Bourride

MAKES 4 SERVINGS

This quick version of bourride, a Mediterranean seafood soup similar to bouillabaisse, nets unforgettable flavor from garlic and orange peel.

2 tablespoons olive oil

4 teaspoons minced garlic

1 cup sliced leeks

1 cup sliced carrots

pinch saffron threads

1 can (11 ounces) clam juice

2 cups dry white wine

1/4 teaspoon freshly ground black pepper

3/4 pound flounder, cut into bite-size pieces

1/2 teaspoon orange peel

4 slices French bread, toasted

- Heat the olive oil in a 6-quart pot. Sauté the garlic and leeks until leeks are wilted, 3 to 5 minutes.

- Add the carrots, saffron, clam juice, wine, and pepper. Cover the pot, and bring the mixture to a boil. Reduce the heat, and simmer until the carrots are tender, about 15 minutes.

- Add the flounder and orange peel, and simmer for 10 minutes more. Serve with the bread.

PREP TIME: 10 MINUTES   COOK TIME: 20 MINUTES

Shark Soup with Okra

MAKES 4 SERVINGS

Next time you grill up a flavorful shark steak, save a piece for this soup—it's different and delicious.

2 cans (14 ounces each) fat-free chicken broth

2 medium potatoes, peeled and cut into
   1/2-inch cubes

1 large onion, chopped

2 teaspoons reduced-sodium soy sauce

1/4 teaspoon freshly ground black pepper

1/4 pound black tip shark steak, cooked and
   cut into 1/2-inch cubes

8 ounces whole fresh (or frozen and thawed)
   okra, sliced 1/2-inch thick

1/2 cup frozen peas

snipped fresh parsley, for garnish

● Combine the broth, potatoes, onion, soy sauce, and pepper in a 6-quart pot. Cover the pot, and bring the mixture to a boil. Reduce the heat, and simmer for 12 minutes.

● Stir in the shark, okra, and peas. Cover and simmer 6 minutes more. Serve garnished with parsley.

COOKS' TIP:

When slicing okra, discard the stem ends.

PREP TIME: 10 MINUTES   COOK TIME: 45 MINUTES

Shrimp-Rice Soup

MAKES 4 SERVINGS

A generous splash of lime gives this simple soup a refreshing twist.

2 cans (14 ounces each) fat-free chicken broth

1 small onion, finely chopped

1 celery stalk, thinly sliced

1/4 cup uncooked brown rice

1/2 pound medium shrimp, shelled, deveined,
   and cut into thirds

1/8 teaspoon crushed red pepper flakes

1 tablespoon grated lime peel

juice of 1 lime

● Pour the chicken broth into a 6-quart pot; add the onion, celery, and brown rice. Cover the pot, and bring the mixture to a boil. Reduce the heat and simmer until the rice is tender, about 40 minutes.

● Stir in the shrimp and simmer until they are pink and cooked through, about 5 minutes. Stir in the pepper flakes, lime peel, and lime juice.

COOKS' TIPS:

● Supermarket running a sale on salad shrimp? (Those are the itty-bitty ones in which about 100 equal a pound; by contrast, there are about 35 medium shrimp in a pound.) If you want, you can switch to the miniatures in this recipe; just don't cut them into thirds.

● No time for shelling and deveining shrimp? Then pick up cleaned and cooked shrimp at the market, and cut the final cooking time to 3 minutes.

PREP TIME: 5 MINUTES   COOK TIME: 25 MINUTES

Teriyaki, Snow Pea & Scallop Soup

MAKES 4 SERVINGS

Here's a light and delightful Asian-style soup with an unforgettable balance of complex flavors—snow peas and scallops seasoned with gingerroot, garlic, teriyaki sauce, and Marsala.

2 cups water

2 cups vegetable broth

1 tablespoon grated gingerroot

4 cloves garlic, crushed

1 teaspoon peanut oil

2 teaspoons teriyaki sauce

1 tablespoon Marsala wine

1/4 pound snow peas

1 pound bay scallops

2 scallions, sliced

1/4 teaspoon lemon pepper

- Combine the water, broth, gingerroot, and garlic in a 6-quart pot. Cover the pot, and bring the mixture to a boil. Reduce the heat, and simmer for 15 minutes.

- Stir in the oil, teriyaki sauce, and Marsala. Cover the pot, and return the mixture to a boil. Add the snow peas, and cook for 1 minute. Stir in the scallops, scallions, and lemon pepper, and simmer until the peas are crisp and tender and the scallops are done, about 3 minutes.

COOKS' TIP:

Take care not to overcook scallops or they will become tough and rubbery. Scallops are done when they are opaque from top to bottom.

PREP TIME: 5 MINUTES   COOK TIME: 30 MINUTES

Sherried Scallop Soup with Havarti

MAKES 4 SERVINGS

Here's a rich restaurant-style soup that's easy enough to make at home and fast enough to prepare on weeknights. I'm sure you'll agree that the blend of scallops, cream sherry, and Havarti cheese is magnificent.

2 cans (11 ounces each) clam juice

1/2 cup water

2 potatoes, peeled and cut into 1/2-inch cubes

1 medium onion, chopped

2 bay leaves

1/2 cup cream sherry

1/2 cup shredded creamy Havarti cheese

1 pound bay scallops

1/2 cup 2% milk

1/4 cup snipped fresh chives

• Combine the clam juice, water, potatoes, onion, and bay leaves in a 6-quart pot. Cover the pot, and bring the mixture to a boil. Reduce the heat, and simmer until the potatoes are tender, 10 to 15 minutes. Discard the bay leaves.

• Using a slotted spoon, transfer half the vegetables to a bowl; cover the bowl with foil to keep warm. Add the sherry and Havarti to the pot. Using a handheld immersion blender, purée the mixture in the pot. Return the reserved vegetables to the pot.

• Stir in the scallops. Cover the pot, and simmer the soup until the scallops are cooked through, 5 to 10 minutes. Stir in the milk and heat the soup throughout, about 3 minutes. Top each serving with chives.

COOKS' TIP:

After adding the sherry, cheese, and milk, do not let the soup boil, because it may curdle.

PREP TIME: 10 MINUTES   COOK TIME: 20 MINUTES

Szechuan Shrimp Soup with Cellophane Noodles

MAKES 4 SERVINGS

Got a yen for a slightly spicy soup? Here's an attractive version to try. It has shrimp, bamboo shoots, scallions, sweet red pepper, and cellophane noodles. Chinese chili sauce and five-spice powder give it just the right Chinese character and zest.

*4 ounces cellophane noodles, broken into
    short pieces*
*2 cans (14 ounces each) reduced-sodium
    vegetable broth*
1/4 cup rice wine vinegar
2 tablespoons Chinese chili sauce with garlic
1/2 pound large shrimp, peeled and deveined
1/2 can (4 ounces) sliced bamboo shoots, drained
1 cup sliced scallions
1 sweet red pepper, cut into thin rings
1/4 teaspoon Chinese five-spice powder

- Fill a 3-quart saucepan with water. Warm it over medium-high heat until hot but not boiling. Remove from heat and add the noodles. Soak for 10 minutes; drain.

- Combine the broth, vinegar, and chili sauce in a 6-quart pot. Cover the pot, and bring the mixture to a boil. Add the shrimp, reduce the heat, and simmer until the shrimp are almost cooked through, 2 to 3 minutes.

- Stir in the bamboo shoots, scallions, pepper, and five-spice powder. Simmer for 5 minutes. Stir in the noodles. Simmer the soup for 3 minutes.

COOKS' TIP:

If you can't find cellophane noodles, substitute bean threads or rice sticks.

PREP TIME: 10 MINUTES   COOK TIME: 40 MINUTES

Orange Roughy & Carrot Soup

MAKES 6 SERVINGS

In this enticing soup, a hint of orange makes for a perfect complement to orange roughy. Puréed carrots and diced red pepper complete the flavor balance while giving the dish its eye-catching color.

2 slices turkey bacon

1 large onion, chopped

3 cups clam juice

2 carrots, chopped

2 large potatoes, cut into 1/2-inch cubes

1 sweet red pepper, chopped

2 teaspoons grated orange peel

1/2 teaspoon lemon pepper

1 pound orange roughy, cut into bite-size
  pieces

1 cup 2% milk

COOKS' TIP:

For best flavor, use orange roughy within a day of purchase. In the U.S., it is imported frozen and deteriorates quickly after being thawed.

• Cook the bacon in a 6-quart pot over medium-high heat until browned and crisp. Transfer it to a paper-towel-lined plate to drain.

• Add the onion to the pot, and sauté until translucent, about 5 minutes.

• Stir in the clam juice, carrots, and potatoes. Cover the pot, and bring the mixture to a boil. Reduce the heat, and simmer the mixture until the potatoes are tender, about 12 minutes.

• Using a potato masher, mash the mixture. Bring the mixture to a simmer, and stir in the sweet pepper, orange peel, and lemon pepper. Add the orange roughy, and cook, covered, until cooked through, 3 to 5 minutes.

• Stir in the milk, and heat the soup throughout, about 2 minutes. Crumble the bacon, and top each serving with it.

PREP TIME: 5 MINUTES   COOK TIME: 20 MINUTES

Elegant Crab Soup with Madeira

MAKES 4 SERVINGS

I love crabmeat. Here, my favored crustacean is featured with potatoes, cream cheese, and Madeira in a sophisticated, creamy soup that's at home anytime— at a relaxed Sunday supper, a formal dinner party, or a rushed weekday dinner.

1 teaspoon olive oil

1 medium onion, finely chopped

1 celery stalk, chopped

1 can (14 ounces) fat-free chicken broth

1 large potato, grated

1/8 teaspoon white pepper

1 bay leaf

4 tablespoons fat-free cream cheese

1 can (10 ounces) flaked crabmeat

1 1/2 cups 2% milk

1 tablespoon Madeira

● Warm the oil in a 6-quart pot over medium-high heat for 1 minute. Add the onion and celery, and sauté until the onion is translucent. Stir in the broth, potato, white pepper, and bay leaf. Cover the pot, and bring the mixture to a boil. Reduce the heat, and simmer the mixture for 10 minutes. Discard the bay leaf.

● Stir in the cream cheese. Using a handheld immersion blender, purée the mixture. Stir in the crabmeat.

● Stir in the milk, and heat the soup throughout (do not let it boil). Stir in the Madeira. Serve immediately.

COOKS' TIPS:

- If you have a food processor, use it to grate the potatoes.
- Before stirring the crabmeat into the soup, remove any bits of shell.

Poultry-Plus Soups

Chicken-Ditalini Soup •
with Cannellini Beans

Easy Tortilla Soup with Chicken •

Chicken Noodle Soup •
with Fresh Tomatoes

Chicken Soupe au Pistou •

Chicken Soup Monterey •

Mesquite Chicken Soup •

Quick Matzoh Ball Soup •

• Lemon Chicken &
Wild Pecan Rice Soup

• Smoky Tenderloin Soup

• Winter-White Vegetable & Turkey Soup

• Sweet Italian Sausage Soup
with Peppers

• Asian-Style Turkey Soup

• Harvest Turkey Soup

• Turkey Soup with Acini di Pepe

PREP TIME: 10 MINUTES   COOK TIME: 30 MINUTES

Chicken-Ditalini Soup
with Cannellini Beans

MAKES 4 SERVINGS

Here's a change-of-pace chicken soup. It uses ditalini instead of the usual noodles and adds beans for extra fiber and flavor.

1 teaspoon olive oil

1/2 pound boneless, skinless chicken breast,
  cut into 1/2-inch cubes

1/4 teaspoon freshly ground black pepper

4 cloves garlic, chopped

1 shallot, chopped

2 cans (16 ounces each) fat-free chicken broth

1 can (15 ounces) cannellini beans, rinsed and
  drained

2 carrots, thinly sliced

1 celery stalk, thinly sliced

2 bay leaves

1 sprig fresh lemon thyme

3/4 cup ditalini (tube pasta)

● Warm the oil in a 6-quart pot over medium-high heat for 1 minute. Coat the chicken with the pepper. Add chicken, garlic, and shallots to the pot, and sauté until the chicken is lightly browned, about 5 minutes.

● Stir in the broth, beans, carrots, celery, bay leaves, and lemon thyme. Cover the pot, and bring the mixture to a boil. Reduce the heat, and simmer for 10 minutes. Stir in the ditalini and cook the soup until the pasta is al dente, 10 to 12 minutes. Discard the bay leaves.

> **COOKS' TIP:**
>
> Can't find any fresh lemon thyme? Use regular thyme and add 1/4 teaspoon lemon peel.

12-2-13: Gets an 8. Very flavorful. Better with Parmesan cheese. Suggest meat from roasted chicken - probably thigh. Total time was 1 1/2 hours. Might try adding lemon at the end.

PREP TIME: 10 MINUTES   COOK TIME: 30 MINUTES

Easy Tortilla Soup with Chicken

MAKES 4 SERVINGS

I first savored this nippy soup during a quick trip to Mexico City. This version includes chicken and tomatoes, and is hearty enough to be a meal in itself.

1 teaspoon olive oil

1 pound boneless, skinless chicken breasts, cut into 1/2-inch cubes

2 medium onions, finely chopped

4 cloves garlic, minced

4 cups crushed tomatoes

3 cups chicken broth

1 yellow chili pepper, seeded and minced

2 tablespoons snipped fresh parsley

8 baked tortilla chips, crushed

3/4 cup shredded Monterey Jack cheese

● Warm the oil in a 6-quart pot over medium-high heat for 1 minute. Add the chicken, onions, and garlic, and sauté until the chicken is browned and the onions are translucent, 5 to 6 minutes.

● Stir in the tomatoes, broth, pepper, and parsley. Cover the pot, and bring the mixture to a boil. Reduce the heat, and simmer for 20 minutes. Top each serving with the tortilla chips and Monterey Jack cheese.

COOKS' TIP:

To make your own baked tortilla chips, cut 2 flour or corn tortillas into 1-inch-wide strips. Place the strips on a baking sheet and mist them with cooking spray. Broil them until they're lightly browned, 3 to 5 minutes.

PREP TIME: 15 MINUTES   COOK TIME: 25 MINUTES

Chicken Noodle Soup with Fresh Tomatoes

MAKES 4 SERVINGS

Carrots reign in many traditional chicken-noodle soups; here, tomatoes rule. I think you'll like the perky, unconventional touch.

2 pounds ripe tomatoes

1 teaspoon olive oil

3/4 pound boneless, skinless chicken breasts,
   cut into 1/2-inch chunks

1/4 teaspoon white pepper

1 teaspoon thyme leaves

4 cloves garlic, crushed

1 can (14 ounces) fat-free chicken broth

1 teaspoon white wine vinegar

1 cup medium egg noodles

1 cup frozen peas

- Peel and seed the tomatoes, reserving the juice. Cut the tomatoes into small chunks.

- Warm the oil in a 6-quart pot over medium-high heat. Coat the chicken with the pepper, thyme, and garlic. Add the chicken to the pot, and sauté until the pieces are lightly browned, about 5 minutes.

- Stir in the broth, vinegar, and tomatoes. Cover the pot, and bring the mixture to a boil. Reduce the heat, and simmer for 10 minutes. Add the reserved tomato juice if the soup is too thick.

- Stir in the noodles and peas, and cook until the noodles are al dente and the peas are tender, about 5 minutes.

COOKS' TIP:

For directions on peeling and seeding tomatoes, see Cooks' Tips under Chunky Cream of Tomato Soup with Tarragon (page 123).

Chicken Soupe au Pistou

MAKES 6 SERVINGS

True to its Provençale heritage, this vegetable-packed chicken soup gets its wonderful garlic flavor from pistou, the French version of the Italian pesto sauce.

2 cans (14 ounces each) fat-free chicken broth

3/4 pound boneless, skinless chicken breasts,
   cut into 1/2-inch cubes

1 large potato, cut into 1/2-inch cubes

2 carrots, diced

1 leek, white part only, thinly sliced

1/4 teaspoon white pepper

1 tomato, quartered and sliced

1 medium zucchini, quartered and sliced

1/4 cup grated Romano cheese

PISTOU

1/4 cup snipped fresh basil

4 cloves garlic, crushed

2 teaspoons olive oil

- Combine the broth, chicken, potato, carrots, leek, and pepper in a 6-quart pot. Cover the pot, and bring the mixture to a boil. Reduce the heat, and simmer the mixture for 12 minutes.

- In the meantime, make the pistou: Combine the basil, garlic, and oil in a small bowl.

- Add the tomato and zucchini to the chicken mixture in the pot, and simmer for 10 minutes. Stir in the pistou. Top each serving with the Romano cheese.

COOKS' TIP:

Purple basil, if it's available to you, looks very pretty in this soup.

Chicken Soup Monterey

MAKES 4 SERVINGS

Definitely not your run-of-the-mill chicken soup. This version is spiked with smoky mesquite flavoring, and it's got a noticeably rich broth—thanks to Monterey Jack cheese. But don't fret—it's still low in calories, fat, and sodium. Best of all, its flavor is incomparable.

2 cans (14 ounces each) fat-free chicken broth

2 large potatoes, peeled and cubed

1 celery stalk, sliced

2 carrots, sliced

1 medium onion, chopped

2 ounces deli smoked chicken breast, diced

1/2 cup snipped fresh parsley

1/2 teaspoon dried marjoram leaves

1/2 teaspoon freshly ground black pepper

2/3 cup shredded reduced-fat Monterey Jack cheese

1 teaspoon mesquite smoke flavoring

● Combine the broth, potatoes, celery, carrots, onion, chicken, parsley, marjoram, and pepper in a 6-quart pot. Cover the pot, and bring the mixture to a boil. Reduce the heat, and simmer until the vegetables are tender, about 15 minutes.

● Remove from the heat and stir in the cheese and smoke flavoring.

PREP TIME: 10 MINUTES   COOK TIME: 25 MINUTES

Mesquite Chicken Soup

MAKES 4 SERVINGS

Green tomatoes are the surprise ingredient in this Southwest-inspired soup. Serve it often; it can be prepared in a flash.

2 teaspoons olive oil

3/4 pound boneless, skinless chicken breasts, cut into 1/2-inch cubes

1 medium onion, chopped

2 cans (14 ounces each) fat-free chicken broth

1/2 pound green tomatoes, quartered and sliced

1/2 cup canned black beans, rinsed and drained

1/2 cup canned pinto beans, rinsed and drained

1 small mild green chili, chopped

1/2 teaspoon cumin seeds

1/4 teaspoon freshly ground black pepper

1 teaspoon mesquite smoke flavoring

1/4 cup snipped fresh sage

• Warm the oil in a 6-quart pot over medium-high heat for 1 minute. Add the chicken and onion, and sauté until the chicken is lightly browned, about 6 minutes. Stir in the broth, tomatoes, black beans, pinto beans, chili, cumin, and black pepper. Cover the pot, and bring the mixture to a boil. Reduce the heat, and simmer for 15 minutes.

• Stir in the mesquite flavoring. Top each serving with the sage.

COOKS' TIP:

Chilies that would be good in this soup include Anaheim and Serrano.

PREP TIME: 5 MINUTES, PLUS CHILLING   COOK TIME: 25 MINUTES

Quick Matzoh Ball Soup

MAKES 4 SERVINGS

Matzoh ball soup is traditionally enjoyed at the Passover seder, but it's a treat anytime. This version is delicately seasoned with nutmeg and fresh parsley and is quick to prepare.

1/2 cup fat-free egg substitute, lightly beaten

1 teaspoon olive oil

2 tablespoons water

1/2 teaspoon dried minced onion

1/8 teaspoon nutmeg

1 tablespoon minced fresh parsley

1/8 teaspoon white pepper

1/2 cup matzoh meal

4 cups fat-free chicken broth

- Combine the egg substitute, oil, water, onion, nutmeg, parsley, and pepper in a bowl. Add the matzoh meal and mix well. Cover the bowl, and refrigerate for 15 minutes.

- Meanwhile, bring the broth to a simmer in a 6-quart pot.

- Form the matzoh mixture into 1-inch balls. Drop the balls into the broth and cook for 20 minutes.

PREP TIME: 10 MINUTES   COOK TIME: 35 MINUTES

Lemon Chicken & Wild Pecan Rice Soup

MAKES 4 SERVINGS

A twist of lemon gives this fuss-free and fast chicken soup a fresh and updated taste.

2 cans (14 ounces each) fat-free chicken broth

1/2 pound boneless, skinless chicken breasts, cut into 1/2-inch cubes

1/2 cup wild pecan rice

1 celery stalk, thinly sliced

1 medium onion, cut into thin wedges

1 carrot, thinly sliced

1 teaspoon thyme

1/2 teaspoon grated lemon peel

juice of 1/2 lemon

1/4 teaspoon crushed red pepper flakes

• Combine the broth, chicken, rice, celery, onion, carrot, and thyme in a 6-quart pot. Cover the pot, and bring the mixture to a boil. Reduce the heat, and simmer for 30 minutes.

• Stir in the lemon peel, lemon juice, and pepper flakes. Cook for 1 minute more.

COOKS' TIP:

To get the most from a lemon, first grate the peel; then juice the pulp.

PREP TIME: 5 MINUTES   COOK TIME: 25 MINUTES

Smoky Tenderloin Soup

MAKES 4 SERVINGS

Impress family and friends with this fast, no-hassle soup of turkey, tomatoes, and beans. Its flavors are delightfully smoky and complex, thanks to bottled hickory smoke flavoring.

2 teaspoons canola oil

1 pound turkey tenderloin, cut into short strips

1 medium red onion, chopped

2 cans (14 ounces each) fat-free chicken broth

1 can (15 ounces) great northern beans, rinsed
　and drained

1 can (15 ounces) diced tomatoes

2 stalks celery, sliced

2 teaspoons white wine vinegar

1/4 teaspoon white pepper

1 teaspoon hickory smoke flavoring

1/2 cup snipped fresh cilantro

• Warm the oil in a 6-quart pot over medium-high heat for 1 minute. Add the turkey and onion, and sauté until the strips are lightly browned, about 5 minutes.

• Stir in the broth, beans, tomatoes, celery, vinegar, and pepper. Cover the pot, and bring the mixture to a boil. Reduce the heat, and simmer until the vegetables are tender and the turkey is cooked through, about 15 minutes.

• Stir in the smoke flavoring. Top each serving with the cilantro.

COOKS' TIP:

If your market is out of turkey tenderloin, substitute turkey cutlets or slices.

Winter-White Vegetable & Turkey Soup

MAKES 6 SERVINGS

Got some potatoes, turnips, white beans, and leftover roast turkey breast? Turn them into this tantalizing soup. For color and texture contrasts, serve it with a crisp green salad and crunchy croutons.

1 teaspoon olive oil

1 medium onion, chopped

4 cloves garlic, chopped

2 cans (14 ounces each) fat-free chicken broth

2 potatoes, peeled and cut into 1/2-inch cubes

1 white turnip, peeled and cut into 1/2-inch cubes

1 small yellow squash, quartered lengthwise
   and sliced

1 can (15 ounces) cannellini beans, rinsed
   and drained

1/4 pound cooked turkey breast, cut into 1-inch cubes

1/4 teaspoon white pepper

1 teaspoon dried basil leaves

snipped parsley, for garnish

• Warm the oil in a 6-quart pot over medium-high heat for 1 minute. Add the onion and garlic and sauté them until the onion begins to brown. Pour in the broth.

• Stir in the potatoes, turnip, squash, beans, turkey, pepper, and basil. Cover the pot, and bring the mixture to a boil. Reduce the heat, and simmer until the vegetables are tender, 15 to 18 minutes.

• Remove the pot from the heat. Using a slotted spoon, transfer half the vegetables and turkey to a bowl. Cover the bowl with foil to keep the ingredients warm.

• Using a handheld immersion blender, purée the vegetables and turkey in the pot. Return the reserved vegetables and turkey to the pot. Serve the soup garnished with parsley.

COOKS' TIP:

If you don't have leftover turkey, use deli turkey.

PREP TIME: 10 MINUTES   COOK TIME: 40 MINUTES

Sweet Italian Sausage Soup with Peppers

MAKES 6 SERVINGS

Can't decide whether to have a sausage and pepper sandwich or a heartwarming soup? Then have the best of each. This smart soup is packed with flavor and brimming with sausage, tomatoes, and colorful peppers.

1/2 *pound sweet Italian turkey sausage, sliced*

1 *large onion, chopped*

2 *cloves garlic, minced*

2 *cans (14 ounces each) fat-free chicken broth*

1/2 *pound red potatoes, chopped*

1/2 *teaspoon fennel seeds*

1/4 *teaspoon freshly ground black pepper*

1 *can (14 ounces) stewed tomatoes, cut up*

1/2 *sweet green pepper, chopped*

1/2 *yellow pepper, chopped*

● Warm a nonstick skillet over medium-high heat for 1 minute. Add the sausage, and cook for 10 minutes. Add the onion and garlic, and sauté until the onion is translucent, about 3 minutes. Transfer the sausage, onion, and garlic to a 6-quart pot.

● Stir in the broth, potatoes, fennel seeds, and black pepper. Cover the pot, and bring the mixture to a boil. Reduce the heat, and simmer for 15 minutes. Stir in the tomatoes, green pepper, and yellow pepper. Simmer soup for 5 minutes.

COOKS' TIP:

Watching your fat intake? Then be sure to pick up a package of Italian turkey sausage. It has much less fat than the standard pork variety.

PREP TIME: 5 MINUTES   COOK TIME: 25 MINUTES

Asian-Style Turkey Soup

MAKES 4 SERVINGS

Chinese five-spice powder gives this exuberant soup its sensational flavor kick. Inspiration for it came from a family-favorite stir-fry. It features turkey, rice, broccoli, and sweet red peppers.

1 pound turkey breast slices, cut into 1/2-inch strips

2 cans (14 ounces each) fat-free chicken broth

1/4 cup long-grain rice

1 tablespoon grated gingerroot

2 teaspoons reduced-sodium teriyaki sauce

1/2 teaspoon Chinese five-spice powder

2 scallions (white parts only), chopped

1 cup broccoli florets

1 sweet red pepper, chopped

● Combine the turkey, broth, rice, and gingerroot. Cover the pot, and bring the mixture to a boil. Reduce the heat; simmer for 15 minutes.

● Add the teriyaki sauce, five-spice powder, scallions, broccoli, and pepper. Simmer the soup for 5 minutes.

COOKS' TIP:

Here's an easy way to store extra gingerroot: Peel the root and cut it into 1-inch-thick slices. Place the pieces in a freezer-proof, self-sealing bag, and freeze. To use a piece, remove it from the freezer, let it thaw at room temperature for 3 to 5 minutes, and mince it. Each piece equals about 1 tablespoon when minced.

Harvest Turkey Soup

MAKES 4 SERVINGS

When only a classic, home-style soup will do, give this one a try. Butternut squash and cloves give it a new twist. A dab of butter adds unexpected richness.

1 teaspoon olive oil

1 pound turkey breast cutlets, cut into 1/2-inch pieces

3 shallots, sliced

2 cans (14 ounces each) fat-free chicken broth

1 cup water

2 medium red potatoes, cut into 1/2-inch cubes

1 pound butternut squash, peeled and cut
   into 1/2-inch cubes

1/2 teaspoon thyme leaves

2 whole cloves

1 teaspoon butter

thyme sprigs for garnish (optional)

● Warm the oil in a 6-quart pot over medium-high heat for 1 minute. Add the turkey and shallots, and sauté them until the turkey is lightly browned.

● Stir in the broth, water, potatoes, squash, and thyme. Place the cloves in a mesh tea ball or tie them up in cheesecloth. Add the cloves to the pot. Cover the pot, and bring the mixture to a boil. Reduce the heat, and simmer until the turkey is cooked through and the potatoes and squash are tender, about 15 minutes. Discard the cloves. Stir in the butter. Garnish with thyme sprigs.

PREP TIME: 10 MINUTES   COOK TIME: 35 MINUTES

Turkey Soup with Acini di Pepe

MAKES 4 SERVINGS

Get ready for some really good eating. This extra-easy soup is a family favorite featuring turkey, pasta, peas, and tomatoes. The turmeric gives it a hint of yellow.

1 teaspoon olive oil

1 pound turkey breast strips

1 onion, chopped

2 stalks celery, thinly sliced

4 cloves garlic, chopped

4 cups fat-free chicken broth

1/8 teaspoon turmeric

1 lemon thyme sprig or 1 teaspoon thyme

1/3 cup acini di pepe pasta

1 cup frozen peas

2 cups chopped tomatoes

1/4 teaspoon freshly ground black pepper

- Warm the oil in a 6-quart pot over medium-high heat for 1 minute. Add the turkey, and cook until the pieces are lightly browned, 4 to 5 minutes. Stir in the onion, celery, and garlic, and sauté until the onion is translucent. Stir in the broth, turmeric, and lemon thyme. Cover the pot, and bring the mixture to a boil. Reduce the heat, and simmer for 10 minutes.

- Stir in the acini di pepe, and cook for 10 minutes. Stir in the peas, tomatoes, and black pepper. Cook until the pasta is al dente and the vegetables are tender, about 4 minutes. Discard the lemon thyme.

COOKS' TIP:

Can't find any turkey breast strips? Then get breast slices or cutlets and cut them into thin 1-inch-long strips.

Beef & Other Meat Soups

PREP TIME: 5 MINUTES   COOK TIME: 25 MINUTES

Beef Noodle Soup Bolognese

MAKES 4 SERVINGS

Ladle on matchless gourmet flavor with this captivating soup. Traditional Bolognese, named after the rich culinary style of Bologna, Italy, refers to a flavorful meat and vegetable sauce that's often served over pasta. This dish simmers the noodles right along with the beef, prosciutto, mushrooms, and tomatoes.

1 tablespoon butter

1 large onion, chopped

2 ounces prosciutto, chopped

1 tablespoon olive oil

3/4 pound ground sirloin

1 cup white mushrooms, chopped

4 cups fat-free beef broth

1 can (15 ounces) diced tomatoes

4 ounces wide egg noodles

2 teaspoons no-salt-added tomato paste

1/2 teaspoon freshly ground black pepper

1 cup garlic croutons

• Melt the butter in a 6-quart pot. Add the onion, prosciutto, and oil, and cook until the onion is golden, about 5 minutes. Add the sirloin and the mushrooms, and cook until the meat is browned and crumbly, about 8 minutes, stirring occasionally. Drain off excess liquid.

• Stir in the broth, tomatoes, noodles, tomato paste, and pepper. Cover the pot, and bring the mixture to a boil. Reduce the heat, and simmer until the noodles are al dente, 8 to 10 minutes. Top each serving with the croutons.

COOKS' TIP:

For directions on making your own croutons, see the Cooks' Tip under French Onion Soup, page 130.

PREP TIME: 15 MINUTES   COOK TIME: 20 MINUTES

Mini-Meatball Soup with Alphabet Pasta

MAKES 4 SERVINGS

Impress hungry diners with this exceptional yet easy soup of meatballs, Swiss chard, and tiny pasta. Provolone cheese provides richness and subtle smoky flavor.

1/2 pound ground round (beef)

1/2 cup quick-cooking oats

3 tablespoons dried minced onions

2 teaspoons oregano

1 egg white

2 cans (14 ounces each) fat-free chicken broth

2 carrots, thinly sliced

2 ounces alphabet pasta

2 cups torn Swiss chard greens

1/2 cup grated Provolone cheese

- Combine the beef, oats, 2 teaspoons onions, 1/2 teaspoon oregano, and the egg white. Form 1/2-inch-diameter meatballs. (The mixture should make about 32.) Warm a nonstick skillet over medium-high heat for 1 minute. Add the meatballs, and cook them until they are brown on all sides, about 10 minutes, turning them occasionally.

- Meanwhile, combine the broth, carrots, remaining onions, and remaining oregano in a 6-quart pot. Cover the pot, and bring the mixture to a boil. Reduce the heat, and simmer for 5 minutes. Add the meatballs and pasta, and simmer until the pasta is al dente, 8 to 10 minutes. Stir in the chard and Provolone.

COOKS' TIP:

Form firm meatballs so they hold together during cooking.

PREP TIME: 10 MINUTES   COOK TIME: 30 MINUTES

Goulash Soup

MAKES 6 SERVINGS

My love affair with goulash soup began 10 years ago in a casual German eatery, and time hasn't dampened my enthusiasm for this robust noodle 'n' beef dish. In this quick version, cocoa and a generous spoonful of paprika give the tomato-beef broth a rich depth of flavor and color.

3/4 pound beef round roast

1 teaspoon olive oil

1 large onion, cut into rings

2 cups sliced white mushrooms

3 cans (14 ounces each) fat-free beef broth

1 can (15 ounces) stewed tomatoes, cut up

1 teaspoon cocoa

4 ounces Hungarian egg noodles (kluski)

1 tablespoon paprika

2 teaspoons caraway seeds

- Trim visible fat from the round roast and tenderize the meat with a mallet. Cut into 1/2-inch cubes.

- Warm the oil in a 6-quart pot over medium-high heat for 1 minute. Add the beef and sauté until it is lightly browned, about 6 minutes. Add the onion and mushrooms and sauté until the onion is translucent, about 3 minutes.

- Stir in the broth, tomatoes, and cocoa. Cover the pot, and bring the mixture to a boil. Reduce the heat, and simmer for 10 minutes. Stir in the noodles and paprika, and simmer for 8 minutes. Top each serving with caraway seeds.

COOKS' TIP:

If you can't find the Hungarian noodles, substitute thin egg noodles.

PREP TIME: 10 MINUTES   COOK TIME: 20 MINUTES

Veal Soup with Mushroom Caps

MAKES 4 SERVINGS

Veal scallops, shallots, white wine, mushrooms—such elegant ingredients plus no-hassle preparation redefine home-style soup. It's light yet satisfying. It's robust yet refined. It's delicious.

2 teaspoons olive oil

1 pound veal scallops, about 1/8 inch thick

4 ounces mushroom caps, quartered if large

2 shallots, thinly sliced

2 cloves garlic, chopped

2 cans (14 ounces each) fat-free chicken broth

1/2 cup dry white wine, such as Chardonnay

1/2 teaspoon white pepper

1/2 teaspoon marjoram leaves

1/4 cup roasted red peppers, chopped

1/4 cup snipped fresh parsley

- Heat the oil in a 6-quart pot over medium-high heat for 1 minute. Add the veal, mushrooms, shallots, and garlic, and sauté until the veal is no longer pink, 3 to 7 minutes.

- Stir in the broth, wine, and white pepper. Cover the pot, and bring the mixture to a boil. Reduce the heat, and simmer for 10 minutes. Stir in the marjoram. Top each serving with the red peppers and parsley.

COOKS' TIP:

When veal scallops are hard to find, substitute very thin slices of veal, and cut them into bite-size pieces.

Quick Vegetable & Veal Sausage Soup

MAKES 4 SERVINGS

A handful of beans, some diced potatoes and carrots, and a little veal sausage. You can throw this hearty soup together in no time flat—no kidding.

2 cans (14 ounces each) fat-free chicken broth

2 medium red potatoes, diced

1 can (15 ounces) cannellini beans, rinsed
   and drained

2 ounces cooked veal sausage, chopped

1 carrot, diced

1 celery stalk, chopped

1 medium onion, chopped

4 cloves garlic, chopped

1/2 teaspoon herbes de Provence

1/4 teaspoon freshly ground black pepper

1/4 cup snipped fresh parsley, for garnish

● Combine the broth, potatoes, beans, sausage, carrot, celery, onion, garlic, herbes de Provence, and pepper in a 6-quart pot. Cover the pot, and bring the mixture to a boil. Reduce the heat, and simmer until the vegetables are tender, about 15 minutes.

● Transfer half the vegetables and sausage to a bowl. Using a handheld immersion blender, purée the soup in the pot. Return the vegetables to the pot. Top each serving with parsley.

Pasta, Peas & Pork Soup

MAKES 4 SERVINGS

This homey soup is a superb last-minute supper choice. The dish uses everyday ingredients and 4 simple steps.

1 teaspoon olive oil

3/4 pound boneless, center-cut pork chops, trimmed
   of fat and cut into 1/2-inch cubes

1 large onion, chopped

4 cloves garlic, crushed

5 cups water

4 envelopes low-sodium beef bouillon powder

1/4 teaspoon ground celery seeds

2 teaspoons Worcestershire sauce

1/4 teaspoon white pepper

1 cup ditalini (tube pasta)

1 cup peas

● Warm the oil in a 6-quart pot over medium-high heat for 1 minute. Add the pork and sauté until the pieces are no longer pink, about 10 minutes. Add the onion and garlic, and sauté the mixture until the onion is lightly browned, about 10 minutes.

● Stir in the water, bouillon, celery seeds, Worcestershire sauce, and pepper. Cover the pot, and bring the mixture to a boil. Stir in the pasta. Reduce the heat, and simmer the mixture for 10 minutes. Stir in the peas and cook the soup until the pasta is al dente and the peas are tender, 4 to 5 minutes.

PREP TIME: 10 MINUTES   COOK TIME: 20 MINUTES

Borscht with Veal Sausage

MAKES 4 SERVINGS

Spicy veal sausage brings zip to this fast version of a traditional Russian beet soup. Serve it hot with a dollop of sour cream.

2 cups canned diced beets with liquid

2 cans (14 ounces each) fat-free beef broth

1 cup shredded carrots

1 cup coarsely chopped red cabbage

1 medium onion, chopped

4 ounces cooked veal sausage, chopped

1/2 cup shredded white turnip

1 tablespoon tomato paste

2 teaspoons red wine vinegar

1/2 teaspoon sugar

1/2 teaspoon freshly ground black pepper

1/2 cup nonfat sour cream

● Combine the beets, broth, carrots, cabbage, onion, sausage, turnip, tomato paste, vinegar, sugar, and pepper in a 6-quart pot. Cover the pot, and bring the mixture to a boil. Reduce the heat, and simmer for 15 minutes.

● Remove the pot from the heat. Using a handheld immersion blender, process the mixture until it is partially puréed. Top each serving with a swirl of the sour cream.

COOKS' TIP:

For maximum black pepper flavor, always use the freshly ground variety. The preground stuff quickly loses its flavor and leaves only its bite.

PREP TIME: 10 MINUTES   COOK TIME: 30 MINUTES

Savory Steak & Sweet Potato Soup

MAKES 4 SERVINGS

Instead of the usual potatoes and carrots, this scrumptious beef soup relies on sweet potatoes for body, flavor, and color. Peas provide a bright burst of contrasting color.

1/2 teaspoon freshly ground black pepper

2 tablespoons snipped fresh sage

1/2 pound round steak, cut into 1/2-inch cubes

2 teaspoons olive oil

1 medium Spanish onion, chopped

2 cans (14 ounces each) fat-free beef broth

2 cups shredded peeled sweet potato

1/4 cup dry red wine

1 cup frozen peas

1/2 teaspoon paprika

● Combine the pepper and sage. Coat the beef cubes with 1 teaspoon olive oil. Rub the pepper-sage mixture over the beef. Warm the remaining 1 teaspoon oil in a 6-quart pot. Add the beef and onion, and sauté until the beef is lightly browned, about 5 minutes.

● Stir in the broth, sweet potato, and wine. Cover the pot, and bring the mixture to a boil. Reduce the heat, and simmer for 15 minutes. Stir in the peas and simmer the soup for 5 minutes. Top each serving with paprika.

COOKS' TIP:

Use the moist, red (deep orange) variety of sweet potato for this recipe.

PREP TIME: 10 MINUTES   COOK TIME: 25 MINUTES

Rustic Lamb Soup with Adzuki Beans

MAKES 4 SERVINGS

Enjoy the classic pairing of rosemary and lamb in this savory soup, which also features potatoes, turnips, beans, and onions.

2 teaspoons dried rosemary

1/2 teaspoon freshly ground black pepper

1/2 pound lean lamb shoulder, cut into
    1/2-inch cubes

1 teaspoon olive oil

1 medium onion, thinly sliced

21/2 cups fat-free beef broth

1 turnip, cut into 1/2-inch cubes

1 medium red potato, cut into 1/2-inch cubes

3/4 cup rinsed and drained canned adzuki beans

1 cup torn sorrel leaves

- Combine the rosemary and pepper. Sprinkle the seasonings over the lamb.

- Warm the oil in a 6-quart pot over medium-high heat for 1 minute. Add the lamb and onion, and sauté until the lamb is lightly browned, about 5 minutes.

- Stir in the broth, turnip, potato, and beans. Cover the pot, and bring the mixture to a boil. Reduce the heat, and simmer until the vegetables are tender, about 15 minutes. Stir in the sorrel.

COOKS' TIP:

To bring out rosemary's delightful piney essence, crush the leaves between your fingers before using them.

PREP TIME: 10 MINUTES   COOK TIME: 20 MINUTES

Chinese Pork Noodle Soup

MAKES 4 SERVINGS

Bok choy, pork, Chinese noodles, sesame oil, soy sauce—all add up to a captivating soup with tons of Asian-style flavor.

1/2 pound center-cut pork loin

1 teaspoon sesame oil

6 mushroom caps, sliced

4 cups fat-free chicken broth

1 tablespoon dry sherry

2 teaspoons reduced-sodium soy sauce

1 cup sliced bok choy

2 cups torn spinach leaves

2 scallions, sliced

4 ounces Chinese wheat noodles

2 cups bean sprouts

● Using a meat mallet, pound the pork to tenderize it. Cut the pork into thin 1-inch-long strips. Warm the oil in a skillet over medium-high heat for 1 minute. Add the pork and mushrooms, and sauté until the pork is lightly browned.

● Transfer the mixture to a 6-quart pot, and add the broth, sherry, soy sauce, bok choy, spinach, and scallions. Cover the pot, and bring the mixture to a boil. Reduce the heat, and simmer for 4 minutes.

● Stir in the noodles and sprouts, and cook the soup for 3 minutes more.

COOKS' TIP:

Can't find any Chinese noodles? Then substitute angel hair pasta.

PREP TIME: 10 MINUTES   COOK TIME 25 MINUTES

Kielbasa with Roasted Pepper Soup

MAKES 4 SERVINGS

Surprise a group of hungry friends with this tasty soup. It's packed with potatoes, onions, and flavorful Polish kielbasa, and topped with roasted peppers.

1 teaspoon olive oil

1/4 pound cooked kielbasa, halved lengthwise and sliced

1 large onion, chopped

2 cans (14 ounces each) fat-free chicken broth

1 large potato, peeled and diced

1 celery stalk, sliced

1 teaspoon white wine vinegar

1/2 teaspoon dried thyme leaves

1/4 teaspoon lemon pepper

1/4 cup diced roasted red peppers, for garnish

● Warm the oil in a 6-quart pot over medium-high heat for 1 minute. Add the kielbasa and onion, and sauté until the onion begins to brown, about 6 minutes. Pour in the broth. Add the potato, celery, vinegar, thyme, and lemon pepper.

● Cover the pot, and bring the mixture to a boil. Reduce the heat, and simmer until the vegetables are tender, about 15 minutes. Top each serving with the red peppers.

COOKS' TIP:

To reduce prep time, replace freshly roasted red peppers with the variety from a jar.

[handwritten: 12/1/15 Supper with Dave + Doris - Beth score 8 out 10 Jim scare 7.]

[handwritten: Very easy soup to make -]

Bratwurst & Beer Soup

MAKES 4 SERVINGS

Here's to a great Germanfest! This lively and hearty soup is perfect for spur-of-the-moment supping, even if you haven't invited a crowd.

1 teaspoon olive oil

1/4 pound cooked bratwurst, halved lengthwise *[handwritten: - could use up to 1/2 lb.]*
  and sliced

2 cups fat-free beef broth

2 leeks, white parts only, sliced

1 large potato, peeled and cut into 1/2-inch cubes

1/4 teaspoon white pepper

1 red sweet pepper, chopped

1 cup ~~nonalcoholic~~ beer

1/4 cup snipped fresh chives

COOKS' TIP:

Before slicing the leeks, wash them in plenty of cold water to remove the sand that's trapped between the layers.

● Warm the oil in a 6-quart pot over medium-high heat for 1 minute. Add the bratwurst, and sauté until lightly browned. Transfer to a bowl; cover with foil to keep the sausage warm.

● Combine the broth, leeks, potato, and white pepper in the same 6-quart pot. Cover the pot, and bring the mixture to a boil. Reduce the heat, and simmer until the potatoes are tender, about 15 minutes. Transfer half the mixture to a bowl; cover with foil to keep the vegetables warm.

● Using a potato masher, mash the vegetables remaining in the pot. Stir in the bratwurst and reserved vegetables. Stir in the sweet pepper and beer. Simmer the soup for 5 minutes. Top each serving with the chives.

PREP TIME: 10 MINUTES   COOK TIME: 20 MINUTES

White Bean & Ham Soup

MAKES 6 SERVINGS

A little white cheddar cheese smoothes out the earthiness of this singular soup. Serve it with croutons or crusty bread to sop up the flavorful broth.

2 cans (14 ounces each) fat-free chicken broth

1 can (15 ounces) great northern beans, rinsed and drained

2 large potatoes, peeled and cubed

1 turnip, peeled and cubed

1 celery stalk, sliced

1 small onion, chopped

2 ounces cooked lean deli ham, chopped

2 cloves garlic, chopped

1 teaspoon white wine vinegar

1/4 teaspoon white pepper

1/4 teaspoon ground dried savory

1/2 cup grated reduced-fat white Cheddar cheese

paprika, for garnish

● Combine the broth, beans, potatoes, turnip, celery, onion, ham, garlic, vinegar, pepper, and savory in a 6-quart pot. Cover the pot, and bring the mixture to a boil. Reduce the heat, and simmer until the vegetables are tender, about 15 minutes.

● Remove the soup from the heat. Using a handheld immersion blender, coarsely purée the vegetables. Stir in the Cheddar. Serve the soup garnished with the paprika.

Zuppa di Giorno

MAKES 6 SERVINGS

Hot Italian sausage and a few pinches of fennel bring intense flavor to this carefree soup. I've used fusilli, but ziti or rotini would soak up the broth's flavors just as nicely.

1/4 pound hot Italian sausage

4 cups fat-free chicken broth

2 cups frozen baby lima beans

2 carrots, sliced

1 large onion, chopped

1 small zucchini, sliced thin

1 bay leaf

1/2 teaspoon fennel seeds, crushed

1/4 teaspoon thyme

1/4 teaspoon freshly ground black pepper

8 ounces fusilli (spiral-shaped pasta)

● Sauté the sausage in a nonstick skillet until browned, about 8 minutes. Transfer it to a cutting board and chop into small pieces.

● In a 6-quart pot, combine the sausage, broth, beans, carrots, onion, zucchini, bay leaf, fennel seeds, thyme, and pepper. Cover the pot, and bring the mixture to a boil. Reduce the heat, and simmer until the vegetables are tender, 15 to 20 minutes.

● Stir in the fusilli. Simmer until the pasta is al dente, about 10 minutes. Discard the bay leaf.

COOKS' TIP:

Got a slow cooker? Here's your chance to use it. Simply sauté the sausage in a nonstick skillet and chop it into small pieces. Combine the sausage and all remaining ingredients except the fusilli in an electric slow cooker. Cover the cooker, and cook on Low for 5 to 7 hours. Stir in the fusilli; cook until al dente, about 40 minutes.

PREP TIME: 10 MINUTES   COOK TIME: 55 MINUTES

Porcini Mushroom & Barley Soup

MAKES 6 SERVINGS

4 ounces pancetta or thick bacon slices, cut into
   1/2-inch-wide strips

1/2 cup chopped shallots

1/2 cup finely chopped carrots

1/2 cup finely chopped celery

2 garlic cloves, minced

2 cups water

2 cups canned fat-free beef broth

1 1/2 cups canned low-salt chicken broth

1/2 cup pearl barley

1/2 ounce dried porcini mushrooms, brushed
   clean of grit

2 large Swiss chard leaves, thinly sliced crosswise
   (about 2 packed cups)

extra-virgin olive oil

shaved Romano cheese

• Cook pancetta in a 6-quart pot over medium-high heat until crisp, about 6 minutes (if using bacon, drain off excess drippings).

• Add shallots, carrots, celery, and garlic to pancetta in pot; cook until soft, about 5 minutes. Add 2 cups of water, both stocks, barley, and porcini mushrooms and bring to a boil. Reduce heat; simmer until barley is tender, stirring occasionally, about 40 minutes.

• Add chard to soup; cook until wilted, about 1 minute. Ladle soup into bowls. Drizzle with oil. Top with cheese.

COOKS' TIP:

If you want to prepare this soup one day ahead, cook the barley, let it cool slightly, and leave off the final step. Refrigerate uncovered until cold, then cover. Before serving, bring to a simmer before adding the Swiss chard.

Index